The Human Body

The Human Body

Organs • Body Systems • Functions

Contents

SKELETON/MUSCULAR SYSTEM 6

| Bones/Cartilage | 8–9 | Skeleton | 10–11 |
| Joints | 9 | Muscular System | 12–13 |

RESPIRATORY SYSTEM 14

| Respiratory Passages | 16–17 |
| Lower Respiratory Passages | 17–19 |

HEART/CIRCULATORY SYSTEM 20

| Heart | 22–25 | Blood Vessels | 29–31 |
| Circulatory System | 26–28 | | |

DIGESTIVE SYSTEM 32

Upper Alimentary Tract	34–37
Lower Alimentary Tract	38–41
Digestive System Glands	42–45

ENDOCRINE SYSTEM 46

Thyroid Gland	48	Genital Glands	52
Parathyroid Glands	49	Pituitary Gland	53
Adrenal Glands	50–51	Pineal Gland	53
Pancreas	51	Endocrine Tissue	53

BRAIN/NERVOUS SYSTEM 54

Central Nervous System 56–57 Nerves 58–61
Vegetative Nervous System 58

SENSORY ORGANS 62

Organ of Touch 64 Organ of Vision 66–67
Organ of Hearing   Organ of Taste 68
and Balance 65 Organ of Smell 69

KIDNEYS/URINARY SYSTEM 70

Kidneys 72–73 Urinary Bladder 74
Nephrons 73–74 Male Urethra 75
Ureters 74 Female Urethra 75

CELLS 76

Cell Plasma 78 Structure of DNA 80–81
Cell Nucleus 79 Metabolism 81

REPRODUCTION 82

Male   Reproduction 88–89
Genital Organs 84–85 Pregnancy 90–91
Female   Birth 92–93
Genital Organs 86–88

APPENDIX 94

Index 94–96

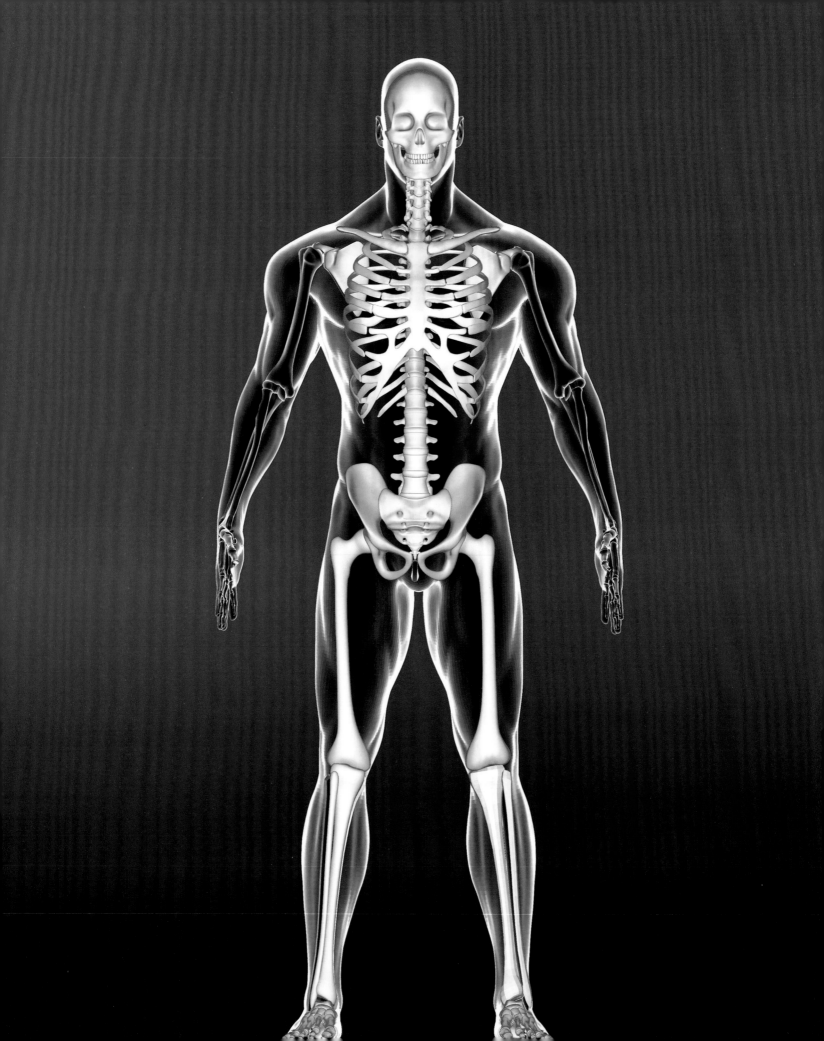

Skeleton / Muscular System

CHAPTER 1

Bones/Cartilage   8–9

Joints   9

Skeleton   10–11

Muscular System   12–13

A visual examination of the human skeleton clearly shows that each one of its 200-plus bones, irrespective of the great variety in shape and size, is merely a component of a long chain. It is the way the parts are assembled, the ingenious skeletal construction, particularly the function of single specialised bones with their special internal structures and their connection to other bones, that really makes a skeleton into the practical, coordinated, functional unit that it is. This unit cannot however function without the aid of muscles and ligaments. The muscles are often combined into larger muscle groups – also referred to as 'muscle slings' – and also participate actively in this complex assembly. Together with the joints and bones, the muscles facilitate complicated movements and allow human beings to build up strength and stamina. Naturally even the slightest movements also require the involvement of the brain, the nerves and the sensory organs in association with the bones, joints, tendons and muscles.

Bones/Cartilage

The skeleton of the human body is composed of more than 200 individual bones that fulfil various functions. Our body is supported by the skeleton, in conjunction with cartilaginous tissue. The skeleton provides both protection for the inner soft parts as well as a framework for muscle attachment. The metabolic activities inside the bones also play an important role (calcium balance, formation of blood in the red bone marrow).

Cartilaginous tissue is found chiefly in the skeleton and the air passages. It is composed of cartilage cells *(chondrocytes)* lying in small groups within a cartilage matrix *(extracellular matrix)*. Depending on the type and number of fibres, cartilage is classified as elastic, hyaline or fibrous cartilage.

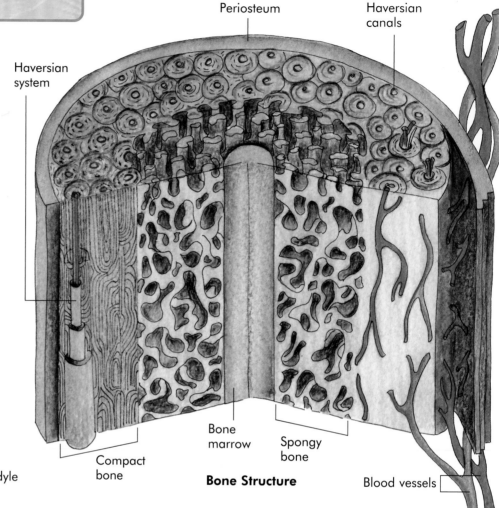

Bone Structure

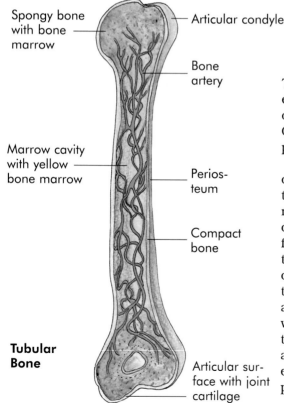

Tubular Bone

The supply of cartilage with nutrients takes place either via the synovial fluid or the perichondrium. Cartilage has a high resistance to pressure and is very robust.

Bone Structure – Bone is an organ composed of various types of tissues. In addition to the predominant proportion of bone tissue, there can also be found fat- and blood-forming (lipogenic and haemogenic) tissue near the bone marrow, firm connective tissue next to the periosteum, cartilage in the growth zones and at the ends of the joints, as well as elastic connective tissue in the blood vessel walls. The bones are supplied with nerves. All bones, except for the joint ends, are completely covered by bone skin, the pe-

riosteum. This is composed of two layers. A bone-forming (osteogenic) layer is immediately adjacent to the bone. This contains numerous osteogenic cells (osteoblasts) during the bone's growth phase, which decrease in number in adults, only resuming activity with renewed cell formation after bone fracture.

The outer part of the periosteum is made up of a network of high-tensile fibres. This provides direct anchorage with the bone and allows the connection of tendons, muscles and ligaments. The periosteum is supplied with blood and lymph vessels as well as nerves. Except for the material making up the teeth, bones represent the hardest substance in the human body.

Bone Formation – Bones can be formed in two different ways. They may either be developed directly from connective tissue (intramembranous ossification), such as for flat cranial bones or the facial bones, or alternatively, bone may replace the cartilage at the ends of the long tubular bones during and after the growth phase. A growth plate (epiphysial disk) is located between shaft and tip of the bone. Cartilage is broken down towards both sides and replaced by bone tissue. New cartilaginous material is however formed at the same time, to allow longitudinal growth. The growth of bone thickness occurs via the periosteum and continues throughout life.

Joints

In order to carry out body movements, it is necessary for bones to be movable while being connected to each other. This occurs via the joints. Joints are classified as monoaxial, biaxial, triaxial to polyaxial, according to the degree of mobility. There are two different joint types. One type is the freely movable or synovial joints *(diarthroses)*, characterised by two bones, the head *(articular condyle)* of one bone within the socket of the other. The second type is the non-synovial joints *(synarthrosis joints)* such as fibrous or cartilaginous joints *(syndesmosis* or *synchondrosis)*. The movement allowed by these joints is rather limited; the effect is to provide a degree of elasticity. Synovial fluid reduces the friction between the articular surfaces. It is located in a joint capsule, the firm tissue of which holds the joint together.

The joints form the connections between the cartilaginous and bony skeletal elements of the human body. They allow movement of the individual sections of the trunk of the body as well as of the extremities. The different types of joints are distinguished on the basis of the structure and shape of the articular surfaces.

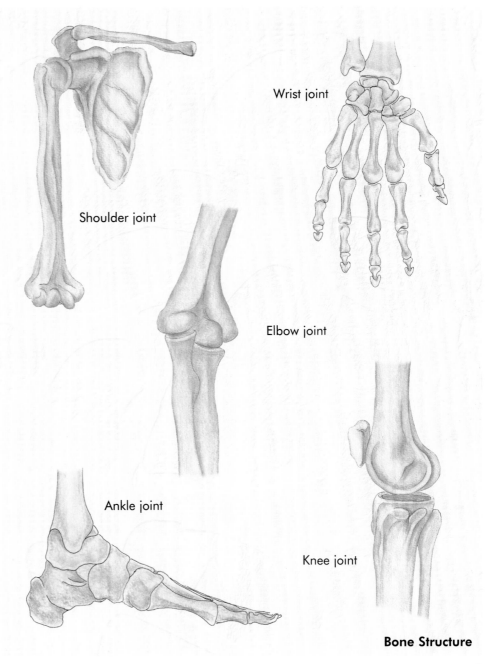

Shoulder joint

Wrist joint

Elbow joint

Ankle joint

Knee joint

Bone Structure

Skeleton

The skeleton is the framework of the body. It is composed of cartilaginous and bony (osseous) elements, which are connected by means of connective tissue structures. The skeletal muscles allow the skeleton to be moved or maintained in a certain position. The skeleton and muscles make up the muscu-

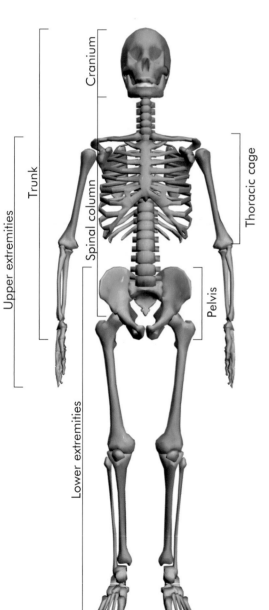

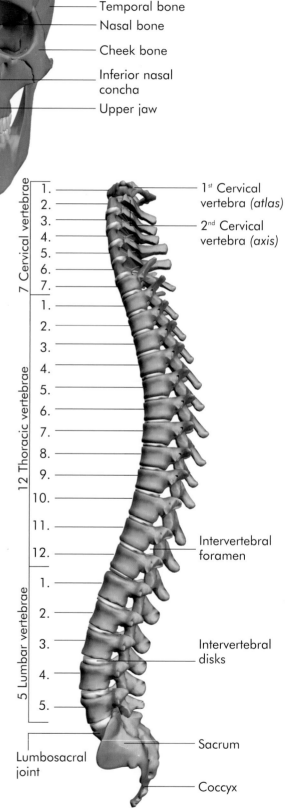

Frontal bone
Sphenoid bone
Lacrimal bone
Ethmoid bone
Nasal septum
Teeth
Lower jaw

Parietal bone
Temporal bone
Nasal bone
Cheek bone
Inferior nasal concha
Upper jaw

7 Cervical vertebrae
1.
2.
3.
4.
5.
6.
7.

1st Cervical vertebra (atlas)
2nd Cervical vertebra (axis)

12 Thoracic vertebrae
1.
2.
3.
4.
5.
6.
7.
8.
9.
10.
11.
12.

5 Lumbar vertebrae
1.
2.
3.
4.
5.

Intervertebral foramen
Intervertebral disks
Sacrum
Coccyx
Lumbosacral joint

loskeletal system or locomotor apparatus.

The passive locomotor system is made up of all of the bones (ossa) and the joints. The skeleton is moved by means of the active locomotor system, the skeletal muscles. The synovial and non-synovial joints link the various bones to each other. They provide support for the muscles and allow fine movements and a large range of mobility by acting as levers. The skeletal elements, skeletal muscles and joints therefore constitute the organs of locomotion.

Skull – The bones of the skull (cranium) protect the brain, eyes and inner ear. Some of these cranial bones provide the framework for upper and lower jaw (maxilla and mandibula) as well as for the eyes, nose and so forth.

Spine – The spinal column (vertebral column) is the central axis of our skeleton. It is made up of a chain of cylindriform bones, the vertebrae, and is very supple yet sturdy at the same time. It facilitates our walking upright, as well as bending forwards, backwards, sideways and also twisting.

Rib Cage – 12 pairs of ribs *(costae)*, joined to the thoracic vertebrae and the breastbone *(sternum)* by joints and cartilage, together make up the rib cage (thorax). It provides protection for organs of the chest and upper abdomen, while allowing a significant volume displacement within the chest during breathing, on account of its flexibility.

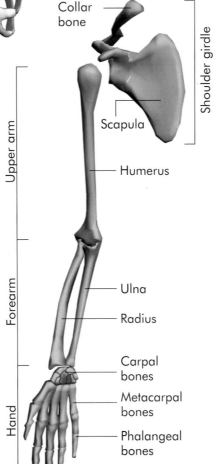

Sacrum
Hip bone
Iliac bone
Coccyx
Pubic bone
Hip foramen
Ischial bone
Pubic arch
Pubic symphysis

1st rib
Sternal manubrium
Costal bone
Costal cartilage
Sternum
Xiphoid process
Floating ribs
12th Rib

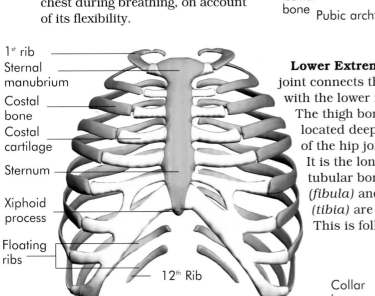

Lower Extremities – The hip joint connects the pelvic girdle with the lower mobile limbs. The thigh bone *(femur)* is located deep within the socket of the hip joint *(acetabulum)*. It is the longest and heaviest tubular bone. The calf bone *(fibula)* and the shinbone *(tibia)* are situated below it. This is followed by the foot,

Pelvic girdle
Upper leg
Femur
Patella
Lower leg
Fibula
Tibia
Foot

Upper Extremities – The upper extremities are joined to the trunk of the body at the shoulder girdle. They are connected via the sternoclavicular joint. The mobile upper limbs starting from the shoulder joint *(glenohumeral joint)* are comprised of the upper arm bone *(humerus)*, the forearm bones *(ulna* and *radius)* and the hand *(manus)*. Important joints such as the shoulder joint, the elbow joint *(cubital joint)* and the wrist *(carpus)* allow a great diversity of movement.

Pelvis – The legs are joined to the backbone via the pelvic girdle, which, in contrast to the shoulder girdle, is firmly attached to the axial skeleton. The pelvic girdle consists of the two hip bones, which, together with the sacral bone, make up a strong ring. This is the part of the body bearing most of the body weight. It supports the body's upright posture and its movement.

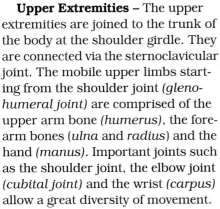

Collar bone
Shoulder girdle
Scapula
Upper arm
Humerus
Forearm
Ulna
Radius
Hand
Carpal bones
Metacarpal bones
Phalangeal bones

which is composed of 26 bones, vaguely resembling the structure of the hand. Its special structure allows us to stand firmly while providing the necessary bounciness required for walking.

An adult skeleton weighs about 10 kg and makes up about 14% of total body weight. The composition of bone – almost two thirds of bone consist of inorganic salts – provides a hard, firm, load-bearing structure.

Muscular System

The muscles constitute the active part of the locomotor system. Their function is to carry out body movements. The muscles make up 40% of body weight. The human body has 300 individual muscles *(musculi)* of varying shapes and sizes. Essential to the composition of muscles are the muscle cells, which are able to contract longitudinally upon nerve stimulation. The muscle cells contain small contractile protein fibres *(myofibrils)*. These shorten on stimulation, while returning to their original shape once the stimulus subsides. Muscle fibres and muscle cells are distinguished according to their structure:

- **Non-striated muscles**
- **Striated muscles**
- **Cardiac muscles**

Non-striated muscles are made up of smooth muscle fibres. They are composed exclusively of myofibrils running along the length of the muscle fibres. This is why the muscle fibre looks smooth and not striped. Non-striated muscles carry out the involuntary movements of the internal organs, such as the peristaltic movement of the intestines.

The **striated muscles** are composed of various tissues. The majority of muscles are made up of striated muscle fibres. All of the skeletal muscles are striated muscles, allowing us to make voluntary movements and participating in the reflexes.

The histological anatomy of the **cardiac muscles** is characterised by striated and non-striated muscles, with single fibril-rich fibres running perpendicular to plasma-rich fibres.

Muscles have a high energy requirement. This can be met by the presence of numerous blood

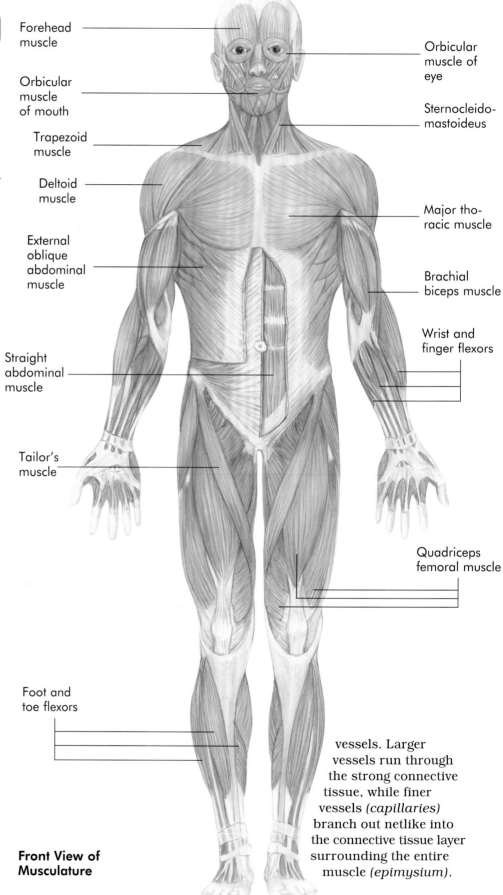

Forehead muscle

Orbicular muscle of mouth

Trapezoid muscle

Deltoid muscle

External oblique abdominal muscle

Straight abdominal muscle

Tailor's muscle

Foot and toe flexors

Orbicular muscle of eye

Sternocleido-mastoideus

Major thoracic muscle

Brachial biceps muscle

Wrist and finger flexors

Quadriceps femoral muscle

Front View of Musculature

vessels. Larger vessels run through the strong connective tissue, while finer vessels *(capillaries)* branch out netlike into the connective tissue layer surrounding the entire muscle *(epimysium)*.

Rear View of Musculature

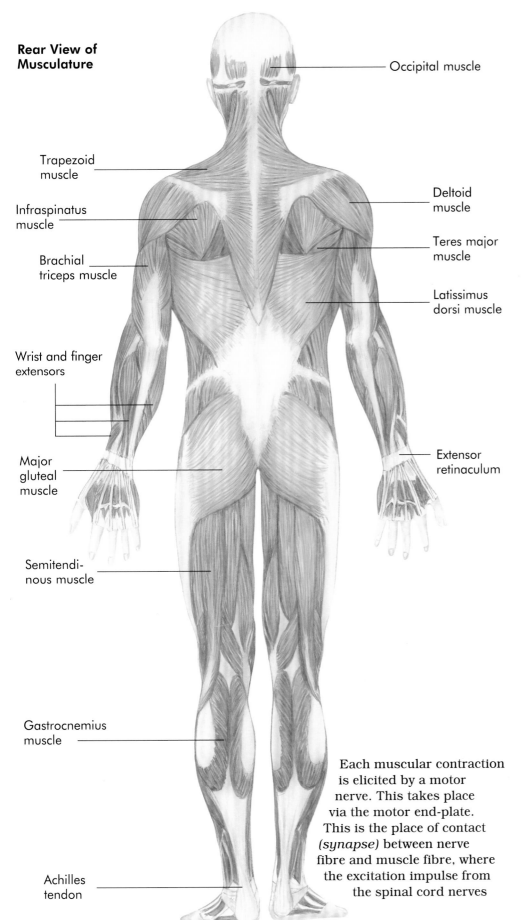

Occipital muscle

Trapezoid muscle

Infraspinatus muscle

Brachial triceps muscle

Wrist and finger extensors

Major gluteal muscle

Semitendinous muscle

Gastrocnemius muscle

Achilles tendon

Deltoid muscle

Teres major muscle

Latissimus dorsi muscle

Extensor retinaculum

Each muscular contraction is elicited by a motor nerve. This takes place via the motor end-plate. This is the place of contact (*synapse*) between nerve fibre and muscle fibre, where the excitation impulse from the spinal cord nerves or brain nerves is transmitted. A single muscle fibre may be supplied at this point or, by means of branching out, even 100 muscle fibres may be supplied simultaneously.

Muscular Function – On entering the muscle, the motor nerves split up into single fibres in order to contact each muscle cell. An electrical impulse, starting from the brain (*cerebrum*), travels along the nerve until it reaches the motor end-plate (*synapse*), which forms the crossing point between nerve and muscle. This excitation is transferred from the nerve to the muscle by means of a chemical substance, acetylcholine, which triggers the contraction of the muscle.

Each muscle fibre (*filament*) contains two different types of proteins (*actin* and *myosin*). These are linked by cross-bridges. A wide-meshed pattern with few cross-bridges is observed at rest. The muscle shortens if the filaments are displaced over each other. Myosin and actin filaments are interlinked, forming more cross-bridges and thereby creating a denser pattern. Once enough muscle fibres have contracted, the entire muscle will contract and the bone (*os*) is moved. The degree of muscle contraction depends on the intensity and frequency of the excitation impulse reaching the muscle. Muscular movement is impaired or paralysed if the connection between nerve and muscle is interrupted.

There are always some muscles that are in a state of contraction. The contractions put the muscle in a state of muscular tension (*tonus*) resulting in body posture. Even the adoption of specific positions by the body (such as standing up or lying down) is achieved by muscle tension, which in turn requires a high consumption of energy.

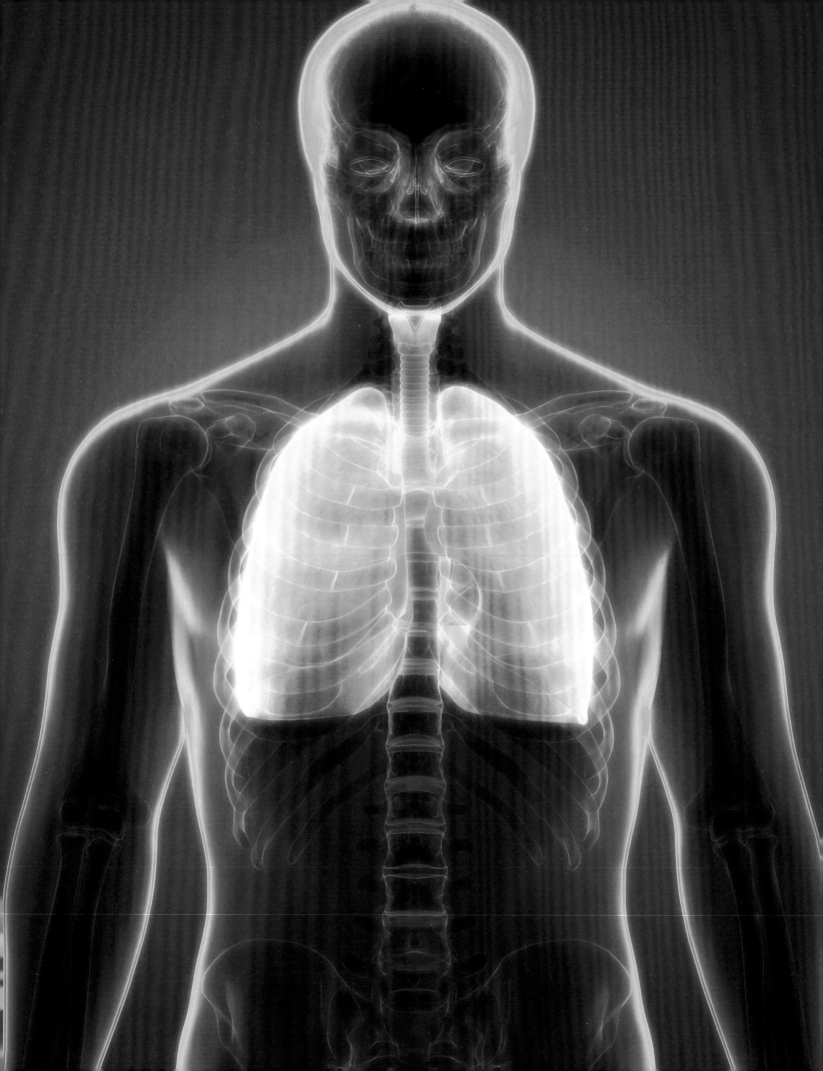

CHAPTER 2

Respiratory System

Upper Respiratory Passages 16–17

Lower Respiratory Passages 17–19

The process of breathing allows the intake of oxygen and the removal of carbon dioxide. This process takes place in the various sections of the respiratory system.

Oxygen is brought to the lungs via the upper and lower airways when inhaling. The cellular waste product carbon dioxide is exchanged for oxygen by the blood of the smallest vessels of the lungs, located in the alveoli. Carbon dioxide is removed from the body by the process of exhalation.

Breathing is an involuntary process. It is controlled from the respiratory centre located in the medulla oblongata. Breathing in *(inspiration)* and breathing out *(expiration)* alternate automatically. The respiratory muscles, composed of the intercostal muscles and the diaphragm, contract during inhalation. This leads to the costal arches being lifted up with a subsequent enlargement of the rib cage *(thorax)*. The ribs are lowered again during exhalation and the diaphragm slackens, resulting in the rib cage becoming smaller again. An adult breathes 12–17 times per minute under normal conditions, while a child breathes about 20–25 times every minute.

Respiratory Passages

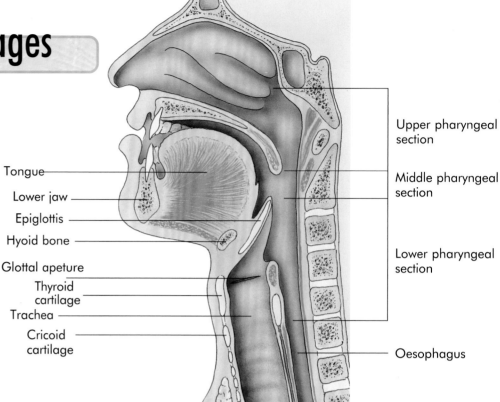

The respiratory organs situated in the head of human beings are referred to as the upper respiratory passages. They include the nose and the pharynx.

Inhaled air first passes through the nose, where pre-cleaning takes place by means of a hair filter. The air is warmed by the vascular network in the nasal mucosa. The air is also moistened by mucus droplets of the nasal mucosa. In this manner, the air is adapted to the conditions prevailing inside the lung.

The air then passes from the nose on to the throat, where gullet and windpipe meet.

The inhaled air reaches the lower respiratory passages via the pharynx.

Tongue
Lower jaw
Epiglottis
Hyoid bone
Glottal apeture
Thyroid cartilage
Trachea
Cricoid cartilage

Upper pharyngeal section
Middle pharyngeal section
Lower pharyngeal section
Oesophagus

Nasal Cavity *(Cavum nasi)*

Inhaled air first passes through the nose, provided we are breathing with a closed mouth.

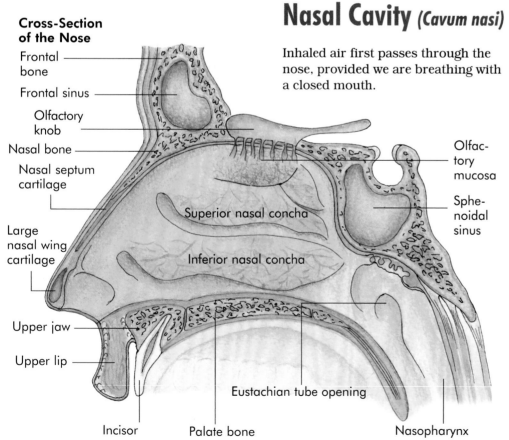

Cross-Section of the Nose

Frontal bone
Frontal sinus
Olfactory knob
Nasal bone
Nasal septum cartilage
Large nasal wing cartilage
Upper jaw
Upper lip
Incisor
Palate bone

Superior nasal concha
Inferior nasal concha
Eustachian tube opening
Nasopharynx

Olfactory mucosa
Sphenoidal sinus

The air flows past a number of bony ridges protruding into the nasal cavity, called the nasal concha or turbinate bones. The well-perfused nasal mucosa warms and moistens the air. The sticky nature of the nasal mucus furthermore helps to remove any dust or dirt that may have been breathed in with the air.

The excretory ducts of the surrounding sinuses (*maxillary sinus, frontal sinus, sphenoidal sinus* and *ethmoidal sinus*) lead to the nasal cavity. Tear fluid is also directed into the nasal cavities from the inner corner of the eye *(canthus)* via the nasolacrimal duct.

Air from the nasal cavity then reaches the pharynx, with the palate, or roof of the mouth, separating the two structures.

The two nasal cavities are in turn separated by the septum of the nose *(septum nasi)*, which is composed of a bony and a cartilaginous part. The front part of the nose is made up of connective tissue.

Pharynx

The pharynx is divided into three sections. The upper section or nasal part of the pharynx, used for breathing, is equipped with mucous membrane similar to that of the airways. There are connective ducts leading to the nasal cavities and the middle ear. The pharyngeal tonsil (adenoid tonsil), which is part of the lymphatic system, is located adjacent to the muscular tube in this upper section of the pharynx, also known as the epipharynx.

The middle section, the oropharyngeal section, is separated by the soft palate. The aperture of the larynx, which is also a respiratory organ, juts into the front part of lower pharyngeal area. Towards the back, it borders on the oesophagus, which is part of the alimentary tract.

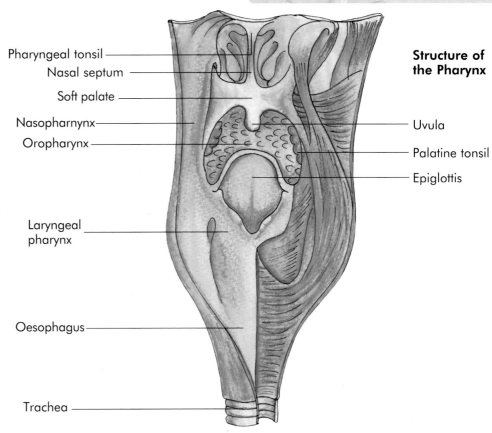

Structure of the Pharynx

Pharyngeal tonsil

Nasal septum

Soft palate

Nasopharynx

Oropharynx

Laryngeal pharynx

Oesophagus

Trachea

Uvula

Palatine tonsil

Epiglottis

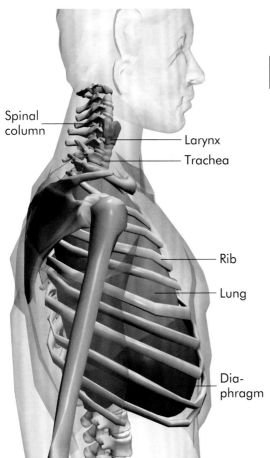

Spinal column

Larynx

Trachea

Rib

Lung

Dia-phragm

Lower Respiratory Passages

The lower air passages include the larynx, the windpipe *(trachea)* and the lung *(pulmo)*.

After the pharynx, the inhaled air passes through the larynx. The larynx can close off the trachea and the connected bronchi from the pharyngeal area, allowing the process of coughing. Air reaches the trachea via the larynx, with the windpipe forming the trunk of the so-called bronchial tree.

Two big branches, the primary bronchial tubes, then continue from here, leading into the left and right lungs respectively. The bronchi branch out into increasingly finer tubes ending in the bronchioles.

Although the diaphragm is not a direct component of the respiratory system, it is the most important respiratory muscle, supporting inhalation and exhalation.

Side View of Thorax
The chest is enlarged during the process of inhalation by the upward motion of the ribs combined with the downward motion of the diaphragm. This results in an increased rib cage volume, allowing the lungs to expand and draw in air. During the process of exhalation, the ribs move downwards and the relaxed diaphragm rises upwards again, with the thoracic cavity becoming smaller again.

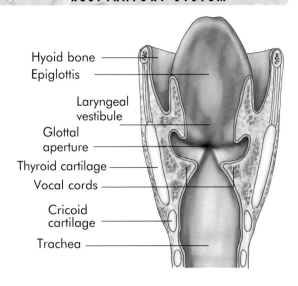

Hyoid bone
Epiglottis
Laryngeal vestibule
Glottal aperture
Thyroid cartilage
Vocal cords
Cricoid cartilage
Trachea

Larynx

After leaving the pharynx, the air passes into the larynx, a cartilaginous structure composed of rings and plates of cartilage, small bones, muscles and small ligaments.

The epiglottis is located at the top. The vocal cords held by the vocal ligaments are situated inside the larynx, running across from front to back. The vocal cords are two mother-of-pearl-coloured mucosal folds, separated by a fissure, the glottal aperture.

The fissure is about 2–2.4 cm long in men, while that of women is a little shorter. The width ranges from 0.5 cm during quiet breathing to 1.4 cm when breathing is accelerated. The vocal cords are adjusted by the action of muscles, also resulting in a change of vocal cord width.

When the gap between the vocal cords becomes very narrow (glottal closure), the air forced through results in a sound similar to a whistle. The oscillations created are transferred as sound waves. Amplification of the sound is achieved by resonance in the oral and nasal cavities. Various sounds are produced depending on the position of the vocal cords, tongue, teeth, lips and the soft palate. This voice production is also known as phonation or vocalisation.

An irritation of the nasal nerve endings, by dust for instance, will automatically lead to a closure of the glottal aperture. The forced expiration subsequent to this sudden closure of the glottal aperture is what we know as sneezing. Coughing arises in a similar manner, by an irritation of the laryngeal mucosa.

These bronchial tubes are known as the bronchi, continuing left and right to each lung.

In addition to the mucous-secreting goblet cells located in the windpipe, there are also cells equipped with movable hairs, the ciliated cells. The hairs, or cilia, are constantly in motion, thereby ensuring that inhaled dust or foreign matter as well as mucus do not reach the lung.

Right middle pulmonary lobe
Right inferior pulmonary lobe

Lung (Pulmo)

The lungs are situated in the thorax, occupying most of the available volume. The lungs are divided into lobes by fissures. The right lung is composed of a superior, middle and lateral pulmonary lobe. The left lung is composed of only a superior and an inferior pulmonary lobe, since space is required for the heart on the left side.

The thoracic wall is covered by a thin protective layer, the costal pleura (pleura costalis). The lung surface is covered by the pulmonary pleura (pleura pulmonaris). There is a narrow fluid-filled gap between the two, the pleural cavity.

This allows the lung to slide alongside the thoracic wall.

The finest branching of the bronchi terminates in the pulmonary vesicles (alveoli). These are equipped with a capillary network. The capillaries are branches of the pulmonary arteries and veins.

Larynx
Trachea
C-shaped cartilage ring
Primary bronchi

Mucous coat
C-shaped cartilage ring
Airway
Muscle layer

Windpipe (Trachea)

The trachea is attached to the larynx. The flexibility of this tube of about 12 cm allows it to participate in the movements of the head and neck. 15–20 C-shaped rings of cartilage ensure that it remains wide open at all times, allowing air to enter unhindered. Behind the breastbone, the lower end of the windpipe splits into two branches.

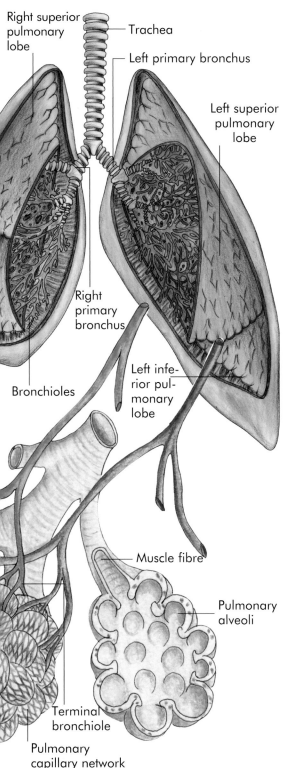

Right superior pulmonary lobe

Trachea

Left primary bronchus

Left superior pulmonary lobe

Right primary bronchus

Left inferior pulmonary lobe

Bronchioles

Muscle fibre

Pulmonary alveoli

Terminal bronchiole

Pulmonary capillary network

Starting from the two primary bronchi, the bronchial tubes branch out into bronchioles, continuing to branch out until they become grape-shaped groups of alveoli. Each of these alveoli, of which an adult has about 300 million, is surrounded by a fine capillary network. This is the site of respiratory exchange. Air containing oxygen enters the capillaries from the alveoli by diffusion. In the other direction, carbon dioxide from the capillaries is transferred into the alveoli, and removed from the lung by exhalation.

The surface of the lung is increased enormously by the alveoli (adults have about 300 million).

This allows gas exchange to take place faster and more efficiently. The alveolar wall is very thin. Depleted venous blood, arriving from the heart, 'charges itself' with oxygen and transports the oxygen-rich arterial blood back to the heart. The heart then pumps the oxygen-rich blood all over the body.

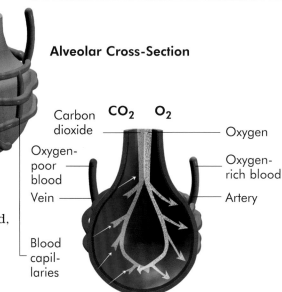

Alveolar Cross-Section

Carbon dioxide

CO_2 O_2

Oxygen

Oxygen-poor blood

Vein

Oxygen-rich blood

Artery

Blood capillaries

Diaphragm

The diaphragm separates the chest region from the abdominal region. It is composed of striated musculature.

The diaphragm both ensures that the abdominal organs are not pushed into the thoracic cavity due to the high pressure (thereby preventing breathing), and is also the most important muscle actively involved in respiration.

In contrast to thoracic or costal respiration, this is referred to as diaphragmatic or abdominal respiration (normal breathing is almost exclusively thoracic breathing). Abdominal breathing involves enlarging the chest cavity and thereby increasing the lung volume, by contraction of the diaphragm.

Very deep breathing may result in a lowering of the diaphragm by 10 cm, the normally convex surface of which then becomes horizontal or even concave. This in turn causes the heart lying adjacent to the diaphragm to be pulled towards the abdominal wall up to the infrasternal (or epigastric) angle. This can be seen with the naked eye on very slim people.

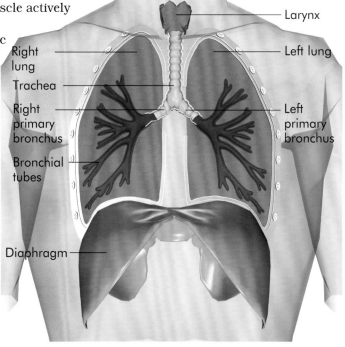

Larynx

Right lung

Left lung

Trachea

Right primary bronchus

Left primary bronchus

Bronchial tubes

Diaphragm

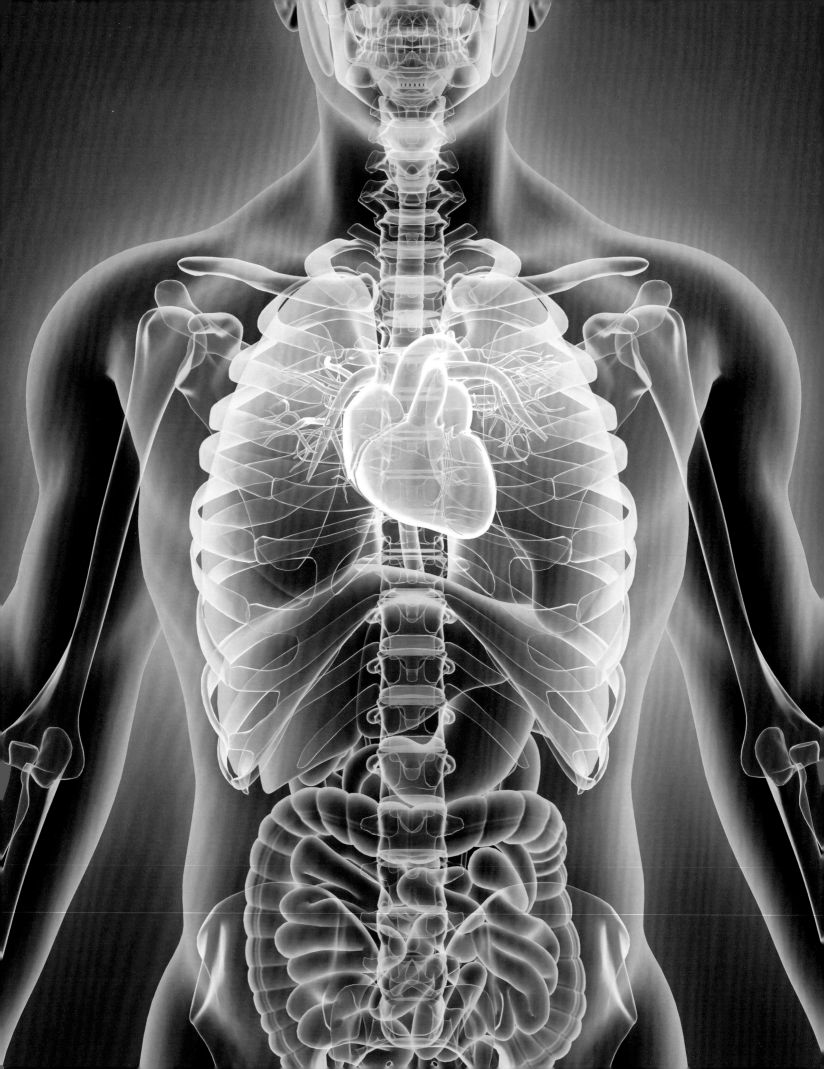

CHAPTER 3

Heart / Circulatory System

Heart   22–25
Circulatory System   26–28
Blood Vessels   29–31

The cardiovascular system is composed of the heart and the systemic (body) and pulmonary (lung) circulatory systems, which in turn consist of a network of arteries and veins. These are necessary in order to maintain the blood circulation essential to life.

The heart, as the motor of the system, pumps the blood into all of the organs and body tissues. In this manner, the blood supplies the body with oxygen, nutrients and other vital substances, while removing metabolic end-products and carbon dioxide. Blood furthermore transports hormones from the endocrine glands to their relevant site of action.

Heart (cor)

The heart is a large hollow muscle approximate in size to its owner's clenched fist and weighing about 300 g. The heart's job is to keep the blood in motion by means of its rhythmic activity.

The construction of the heart ensures that while the ventricles of the heart are contracting *(systole)*, the blood is discharged into the large arteries of the systemic and pulmonary circulatory systems, with blood being simultaneously drawn into the atria from the veins. When the ventricles then relax *(diastole)*, they refill with blood from the atria.

The heart and vessels together make up the cardiovascular or circulatory system, which provides the cells of the organism with all the required substances, while simultaneously removing metabolic end-products.

The heart resembles a cone lying on its side. It is located in the central area of the thorax, almost completely surrounded by the lungs. Two thirds of the heart lie in the left half of the chest and one third lies in the right half.

The inner layers of the wall of the heart are composed of a thin tissue layer *(endocardium)* covering the actual cardiac muscle *(myocardium)* responsible for performing the work of the heart. The outside of the heart is firmly enclosed by a *pericardium*, which connects it to the diaphragm and prevents the myocardial wall from overstretching.

A septum partitions the heart into the so-called 'right' and 'left' heart. Each half is further separated into an atrium (or auricle) and a ventricle (or chamber) situated below it.

The heart is supplied by its own vascular system, the coronary arteries.

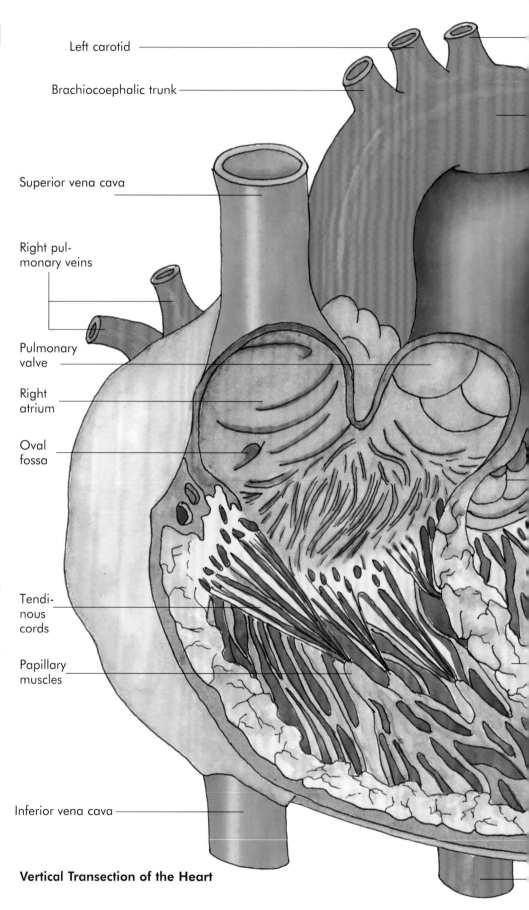

Left carotid

Brachiocephalic trunk

Superior vena cava

Right pulmonary veins

Pulmonary valve

Right atrium

Oval fossa

Tendinous cords

Papillary muscles

Inferior vena cava

Vertical Transection of the Heart

Left subclavian
artery

Aortic
arch

Left pulmonary
artery

The heart contracts up to 70 times per minute, each time forcing about 0.075 litres of pulmonary blood from the left heart into the aorta and the same quantity of venous blood from the right heart into the lungs. It transports about 7500 litres of blood every day, without tiring. This is made pos-sible by a special type of cardiac muscle fibre and the sinoatrial (or sinus) node, a group of nerve cells in the right atrial wall, about the size of a pinhead, which regulate the heartbeat. An increase or decrease in the rhythm dictated by the sinoatrial node is triggered by the cardiac nerves.

**Horizontal Transection
of the Heart**

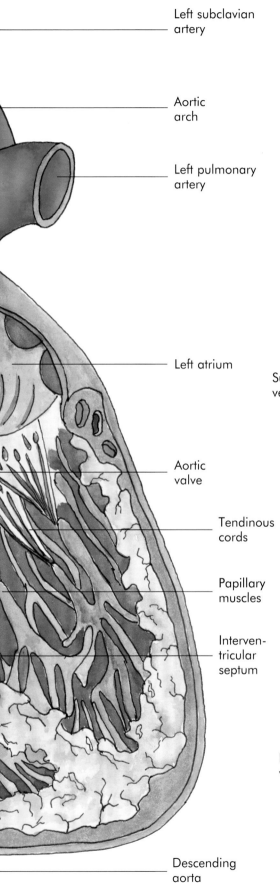

Left atrium

Aortic
valve

Tendinous
cords

Papillary
muscles

Interven-
tricular
septum

Descending
aorta

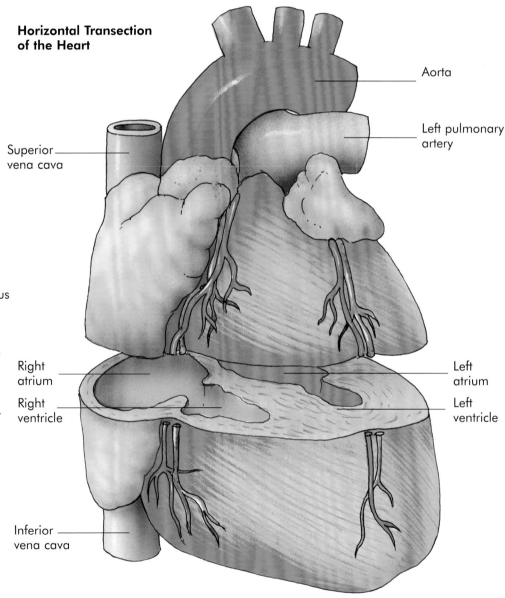

Aorta

Left pulmonary
artery

Superior
vena cava

Right
atrium

Right
ventricle

Left
atrium

Left
ventricle

Inferior
vena cava

The individual compartments in the heart vary in size and in the thickness of their walls. The left heart chamber is surrounded by stronger tendons and muscles than the right one, since it is required to pump oxygen-rich blood into the systemic circulation with enormous pressure.

Ventricles
(ventriculus dextrum, ventriculus sinistrum)

The ventricles are the actual pumps of the circulatory system. The blood is forced into the large arteries by their action. The path represented by pulmonary circulation is much less energy-intensive than that of systemic circulation, due to the smaller overall distance to be covered.

The left ventricle therefore has to operate with a significantly higher pressure than the right ventricle, which explains why the left ventricle is equipped with more muscles.

The septum dividing the heart into chambers, also referred to as the interventricular septum, is similar to connective tissue near the atrioventricular division, but otherwise of muscular nature. A bicuspid atrioventricular valve, also known as the mitral valve *(valva bicuspidalis)* leads into the atrium.

Atria
(atrium dextrum, atrium sinistrum)

In comparison with the ventricles, the atria fulfil less of a pumping function, but act instead as a collecting area for the blood transported back to the heart by the veins.

The muscular walls are significantly thinner than those of the ventricles. A tricuspid atrioventricular valve, the tricuspid valve, separates the right atrium from the right ventricle. A bicuspid atrioventricular valve separates atrium from ventricle on the left side. Both atria are in turn divided by the connective-tissue-like interatrial septum.

Cardiac Valve Systems

There are two types of cardiac valves: the atrioventricular valves and the semilunar cusps (or valves). They prevent the blood from flowing back during systole or diastole.

The atrioventricular valves are located between the atria and ventricles. The atrioventricular valve between right atrium and right ventricle is referred to as the tricuspid valve *(valva atrioventricularis dextra)*, while that in the left side of the heart is called the mitral or bicuspid valve *(valva atrioventricularis sinistra)*.

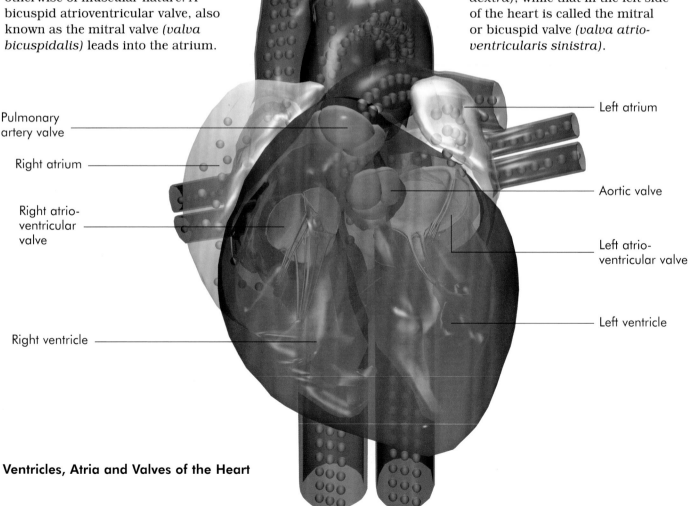

Pulmonary artery valve

Right atrium

Right atrio-ventricular valve

Right ventricle

Left atrium

Aortic valve

Left atrio-ventricular valve

Left ventricle

Ventricles, Atria and Valves of the Heart

The semilunar cusps are located at the outflowing vessels, the large arteries. The right semilunar cusp, the pulmonary valve *(valva trunci pulmonaris)*, separates the right ventricle from the pulmonary artery. The left semilunar cusp, the aortic valve *(valva aortae)*, separates the left ventricle from the aorta. Each half of the heart is therefore equipped with two heart valves, one atrioventricular valve and one semilunar cusp.

The atrioventricular valves prevent the backflow of blood from the ventricles into the atria, while the semilunar cusps prevent the return flow of blood from the respective outflowing vessels into the ventricles.

The semilunar cusps are similar in structure to venous valves. They are each composed of a small membrane attached directly to the wall of the heart. The semilunar cusps lie along the wall when the blood flows in its original direction. They become distended and the edges of the membranes attached to opposite sides come to lie next to each other as soon as the blood starts to flow backwards. The opening through which the blood could flow back up is thereby closed.

The principle underlying atrioventricular valve function is on the other hand reminiscent of a parachute. The valve functions like a small parachute composed of cardiac internal membrane and connected to the papillary muscles by tendinous cords. An increase in the atrial blood volume will cause the parachute to collapse and allow blood to enter the ventricles. Once the pressure in the ventricle increases, the parachute distends and closes the passage from the ventricles to the atria. The papillary muscles and the tendinous cords hold the parachute tight during this process, thereby preventing the atrioventricular valve from opening up into the atrium.

Blood Vessels of the Heart *(Coronary Arteries)*

All tissue, particularly working musculature, requires oxygen. The oxygen requirements of the heart, which is active incessantly, are very high. Although a large quantity of blood is transported by the atria

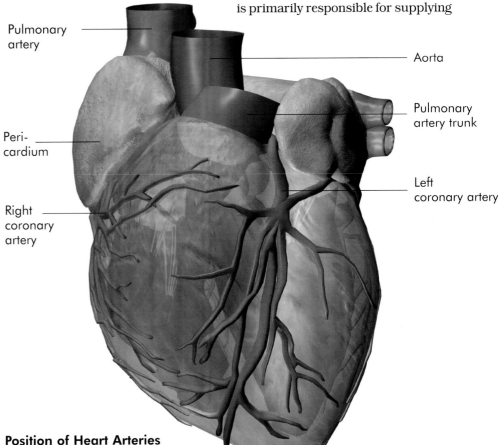

Pulmonary artery

Peri-cardium

Right coronary artery

Aorta

Pulmonary artery trunk

Left coronary artery

Position of Heart Arteries

and ventricles, the heart cannot be supplied from this source.

This is because of the high velocity of the blood stream and also because the muscular walls of the heart are too thick. Therefore, the heart disposes over its own circulatory supply: 5 % of the discharged blood is branched off for this cardiac supply.

The coronary arteries originate just above the aortic valve and encircle the

heart in the atrioventricular groove (or coronary sulcus). This branches out into a fine network of blood vessels, which continues to divide until each cardiac muscle fibre is accompanied by a capillary. The coronary arteries transport about 520 litres of blood through the cardiac muscle every day.

Two branches of the left coronary artery *(rami interventricularis anterior* and *circumflexus)* supply the wall of the left and part of the right ventricle, while the right coronary artery is primarily responsible for supplying

the right ventricle. Both coronary arteries are involved in the atrial supply.

Just as for large circulatory systems, veins are also required here for returning the blood to the heart. The veins carry the blood back from the cardiac musculature and join up to become a larger vessel near the coronary sulcus at the front heart wall *(sinus coronarius)*, discharging into the right atrium.

Circulatory System

Cardiovascular System

Carotid artery and jugular vein

Pulmonary artery and vein

Subclavian artery

Heart

Vena cava

Aorta

Liver

Stomach

Duodenum

Renal artery and vein

Intestinal artery

Blood is the body's most important means of transport. A special, efficient transport route is required in order to supply all parts or cells of the body: this is the circulatory system with its several thousand kilometres of blood vessels.

The circulatory system achieves this task with the help of a pressure/suction pump, the heart, forcing the blood into the large arteries of the systemic circulation, while drawing the blood from the large veins into the atria.

Arteries are the blood vessels transporting blood away from the heart. Their branching out ensures an efficient supply to the organs. The thick walls of the arteries are composed of elastic connective tissue. The arteries are able to convert the high initial pressure created by the heart into an even blood flow in the smaller arteries and capillaries.

The nervous system controls the muscle cells in the arterial walls. On contraction, the diameter of the arteries is reduced and less blood is able to flow through the vessel. This ensures blood supply to all areas in varying situations, for instance providing and storing thermal energy when it is cold, increasing blood supply during exertion and so forth.

The arteries split up into arterioles and continue to divide and branch out into capillaries. These smallest blood vessels are found everywhere in the tissue. Substance exchange with the cells takes place within them. Nutrient substances are supplied while metabolic end-products are removed. The exchange of substances occurs through the very thin capillary walls, which do not represent an obstacle for most substances.

The blood vessels increase in size again after the capillary stage and

The primary object of blood circulation is to transport oxygen, nutrients and hormones, but it also has a protective function for the body, by way of its defence system. The blood is further responsible for the removal of carbon dioxide and metabolic decomposition products.

turn into venules, which first unite to become small and then larger veins.

The large veins transport the blood back to the heart.

The difference between veins and arteries is based on the one hand on their wall thickness: the walls of veins are thinner. Secondly, the

blood pressure in the veins differs from that in the arteries: it is significantly lower in the veins, despite the much larger blood volume as compared with arteries.

The colour of the blood has also changed in the meantime, from bright red (oxygen-rich) to dark bluish red (oxygen-poor, with additional unwanted tissue products and carbon dioxide), and the flow rate is slower.

We distinguish between two circulatory systems, due to the separation of the heart into a 'right' and a 'left' heart: the minor or pulmonary circulation and the major or systemic circulation. The consecutive major and the minor circulations are arranged in the shape of an eight.

Systemic Circulation

The major circulation – also referred to as systemic circulation – starts in the left atrium. Three veins return blood deficient in oxygen but enriched with carbon dioxide and unwanted tissue products from the systemic circulation to the right atrium:

- Venous side of the cardiac circulation *(sinus coronarius)*
- Superior vena cava; collects venous blood from the upper body half
- Inferior vena cava; collects venous blood from the organs and body regions below the diaphragm.

In contrast, the minor circulation only uses one major artery *(aorta)*

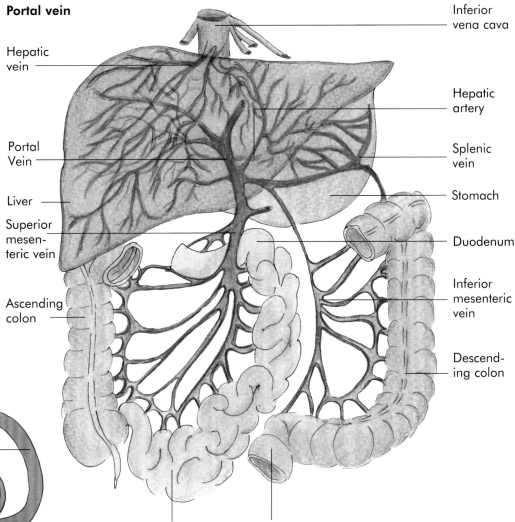

Portal vein

Hepatic vein

Portal Vein

Liver

Superior mesenteric vein

Ascending colon

Inferior vena cava

Hepatic artery

Splenic vein

Stomach

Duodenum

Inferior mesenteric vein

Descending colon

Lower small intestine

Rectum

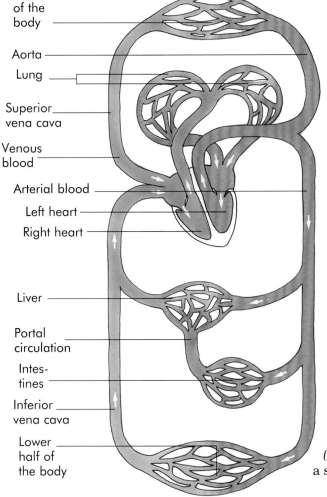

Upper half of the body

Aorta

Lung

Superior vena cava

Venous blood

Arterial blood

Left heart

Right heart

Liver

Portal circulation

Intestines

Inferior vena cava

Lower half of the body

Circulatory System Diagram

for pumping oxygen-rich blood into the body.

Blood from the left atrium passes into the left ventricle via the bicuspid atrioventricular valve. The blood reaches the aorta from there, and is pumped into the body by means of branching arteries, thus ensuring the supply to the head, trunk, limbs and intestines.

A special feature is the supply of the gastrointestinal tract, the spleen and the pancreas. The blood collects in the portal vein *(vena portae)*, which plays a special role. Veins normally

unite to form larger trunks, transporting the blood back to the heart directly. The portal vein is an exception. It splits up into a capillary network in the liver again, from where the liver veins arise. The blood passes through two capillary systems in this case, one in the intestines and one in the liver, the largest metabolic organ of the body, before being replenished with oxygen. Oxygen-rich blood from the hepatic artery is used for the organ's own supply.

The double capillary system is easily explained. Absorbable nutrient substances are broken down in the intestinal capillaries for the purpose of energy generation on the one hand, while toxic decomposition products are transferred to the blood on the other. These decomposition products are detoxified in the liver and do not therefore need to be transported through the entire body beforehand.

The blood from the splenic circulation also flows to the liver, since the decomposition products are also transformed there. The red blood pigment haemoglobin is converted to bile pigment in the liver.

The venous blood from the pancreas is also transported to the liver, since the hormones it contains (insulin, glucagon) influence the carbohydrate metabolism that takes place in this organ (synthesis and breakdown of glycogen).

The excretory products are transported to the kidneys via the arteries, where they are secreted into the bladder, along with plenty of water. The blood is then returned to the circulation after filtration of the excretory products. Approximately 500 litres of blood flow through the kidneys every day, 180 litres of which are filtered by the kidneys.

From the portal vein, the venous blood from the gastrointestinal tract, the spleen and the pancreas passes into the inferior vena cava via the pulmonary veins. The blood from the legs and the lower half of the trunk also joins the circulation here. The blood from the head, arms and upper half of the trunk returns via the superior vena cava. Both venae cavae flow into the right atrium.

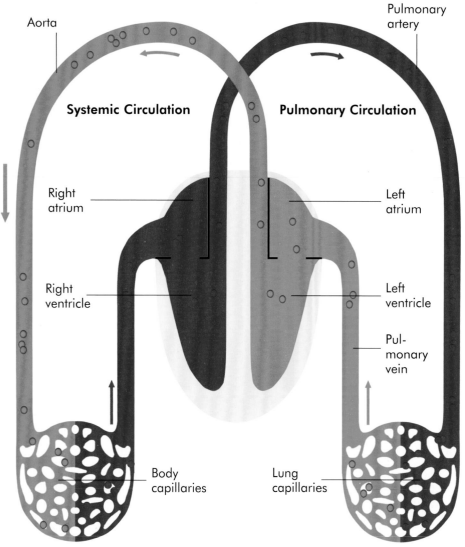

The human body is equipped with a systemic and a pulmonary circulation. While the right ventricle pumps blood into the lung vessels for replenishment with oxygen, the left ventricle distributes the oxygen-rich blood throughout the body.

Pulmonary Circulation

The lung is the only organ involved in pulmonary circulation. Oxygen-deficient (venous) blood flows through the pulmonary arteries into the lungs, while oxygen-rich (arterial) blood flows through the pulmonary veins to the heart.

Pulmonary circulation commences in the right atrium. The blood reaches the right ventricle by way of the tricuspid atrioventricular valve *(valva tricuspidalis)*. The atrioventricular valve prevents the return flow of blood from the ventricle into the atrium.

The blood then continues from the right ventricle through the next valve, the pulmonary valve (valva pulmonalis), to the pulmonary arteries *(arteria pulmonales)* and on into the pulmonary capillaries. This is the site of respiratory exchange. Blood rich in carbon dioxide (dark bluish red) is supplied with oxygen. The arterial (bright red) blood returns to the left atrium via the pulmonary veins *(venae pulmonales)*. The systemic circulation commences from this point.

Blood Vessels *(vasa sanguinea)*

The blood vessels of the body may be classified into three groups: arteries, veins and capillaries. The arteries and veins allow the blood to be transported throughout the body, while the capillaries are responsible for the exchange of substances between blood and tissue.

Except for capillaries, blood vessel walls are composed of three layers, the thickness and structure of each layer varying according to the type of blood vessel. The inner layer *(tunica intima)* consists of thin connective tissue. A layer of simple endothelial cells is located on top of this. The middle layer *(tunica media)* is made up of smooth muscle tissue containing elastic fibres. The outer layer *(tunica adventitia)* consists of connective tissue. It allows structural integration of the vessel into the surrounding region. The layers of the walls of veins are less distinct.

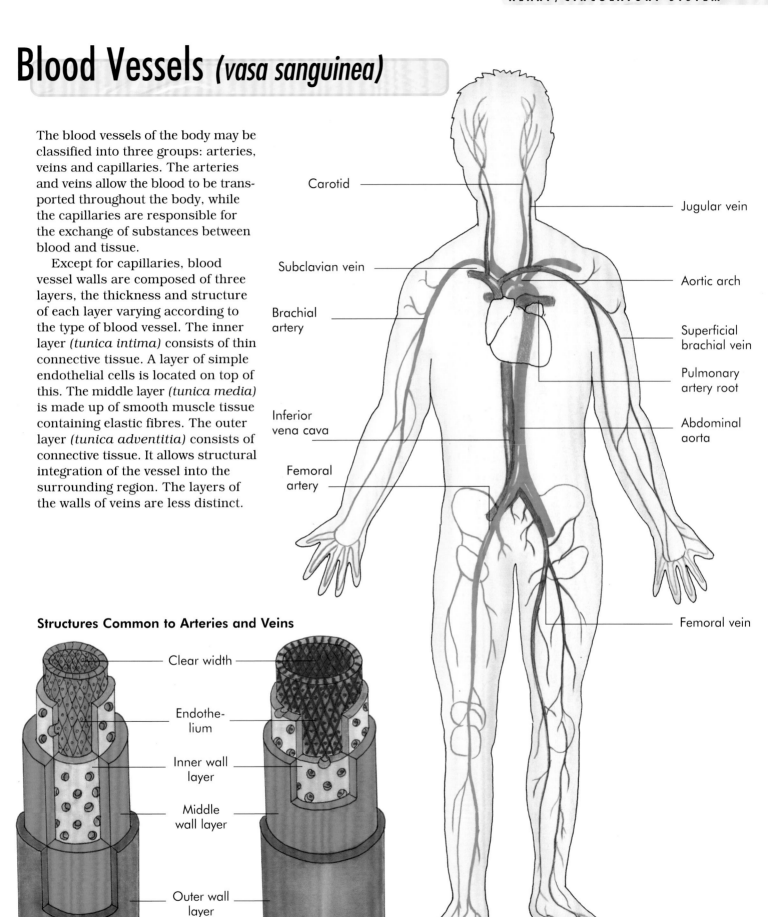

Carotid

Jugular vein

Subclavian vein

Aortic arch

Brachial artery

Superficial brachial vein

Pulmonary artery root

Inferior vena cava

Abdominal aorta

Femoral artery

Femoral vein

Structures Common to Arteries and Veins

Clear width

Endothe-lium

Inner wall layer

Middle wall layer

Outer wall layer

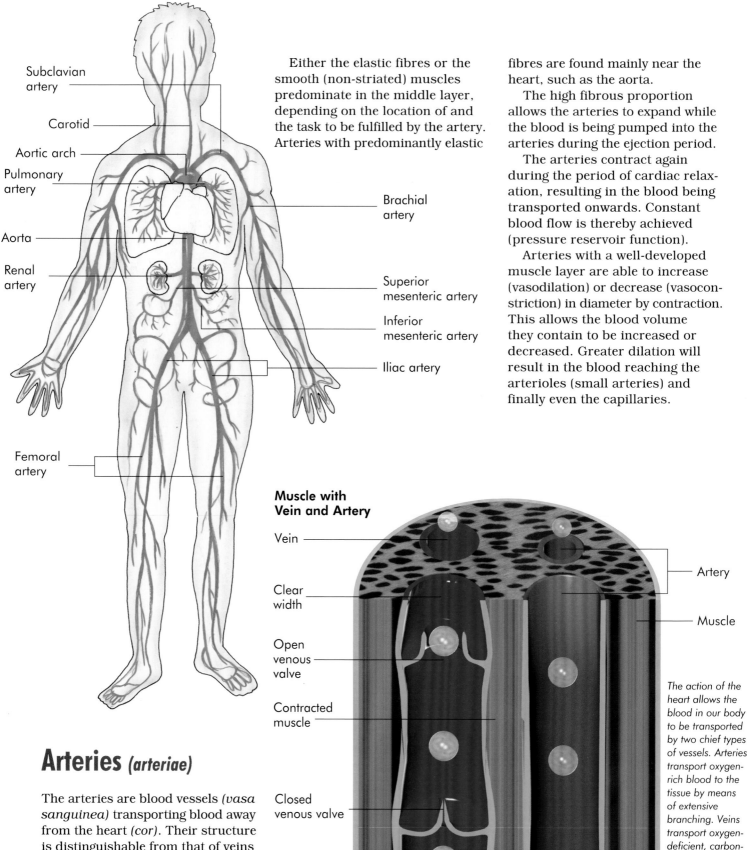

Subclavian
artery

Carotid

Aortic arch

Pulmonary
artery

Aorta

Renal
artery

Femoral
artery

Brachial
artery

Superior
mesenteric artery

Inferior
mesenteric artery

Iliac artery

Either the elastic fibres or the smooth (non-striated) muscles predominate in the middle layer, depending on the location of and the task to be fulfilled by the artery. Arteries with predominantly elastic fibres are found mainly near the heart, such as the aorta.

The high fibrous proportion allows the arteries to expand while the blood is being pumped into the arteries during the ejection period.

The arteries contract again during the period of cardiac relaxation, resulting in the blood being transported onwards. Constant blood flow is thereby achieved (pressure reservoir function).

Arteries with a well-developed muscle layer are able to increase (vasodilation) or decrease (vasoconstriction) in diameter by contraction. This allows the blood volume they contain to be increased or decreased. Greater dilation will result in the blood reaching the arterioles (small arteries) and finally even the capillaries.

Muscle with Vein and Artery

Vein

Clear
width

Open
venous
valve

Contracted
muscle

Closed
venous valve

Artery

Muscle

Arteries (arteriae)

The arteries are blood vessels (vasa sanguinea) transporting blood away from the heart (cor). Their structure is distinguishable from that of veins (venae) on account of an additional elastic membrane layer (membrana elastic interna) located between the inner and middle wall layers.

The action of the heart allows the blood in our body to be transported by two chief types of vessels. Arteries transport oxygen-rich blood to the tissue by means of extensive branching. Veins transport oxygen-deficient, carbon-monoxide-rich blood to the left heart, from where it reaches the lungs.

Veins *(venae)*

Veins *(venae)* are the blood vessels transporting the blood back to the heart. The layers of the walls of veins are thinner than those of arteries, contain more connective tissue and have a less pronounced muscle layer. The diameter of veins is larger than that of arteries. The blood reaches the heart via the veins, having come from the venules *(venula)*, which join the capillaries.

the extremities, are equipped with venous valves *(valvula venosa)*.

The flaps of the venous valves lie along the vein wall when the blood is flowing towards the heart. Venous congestion or a backward flow will result in a distention of the venous valves. The blood is pushed against the closed venous valves and thus prevented from flowing backwards.

Veins cannot transport blood independently because of their thin muscle layer. They are therefore supported by the surrounding muscles. On contraction, these act on the veins like a pump. The diameter of the vein is reduced and the blood is pushed forward as a result. In order to avoid the blood from flowing back, some veins, particularly in

Jugular vein
Subclavian vein
Pulmonary vein
Hepatic vein
Portal vein
Inferior vena cava
Iliac vein

Superior vena cava
Brachial vein
Femoral vein
Great saphenous vein
Popliteal vein
Tibial vein

Capillaries *(vas capillare)*

The capillaries *(vas capillare)* are the smallest blood vessels of the body. They are connected to the arterioles on one end, while linking up with the smallest veins, the venules, on the other. They therefore represent the connection between arteries and veins.

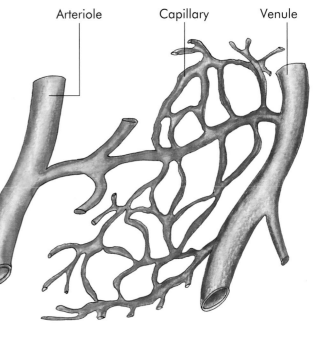

Arteriole   Capillary   Venule

As compared to arteries and veins, capillaries lack both the middle and the outer wall layers. They consist of only one inner layer, made up of connective tissue and endothelial cells.

The very small diameter of capillaries allows the blood to circulate only slowly. This fact, in conjunction with the thin capillary wall, is advantageous for the capillary with respect to carrying out its job of exchanging substances and water with the immediate environment. Blood pressure forces the oxygen and nutrients contained in the blood out of the capillaries and into the intercellular space. Carbon dioxide and metabolic products are reabsorbed in exchange.

31

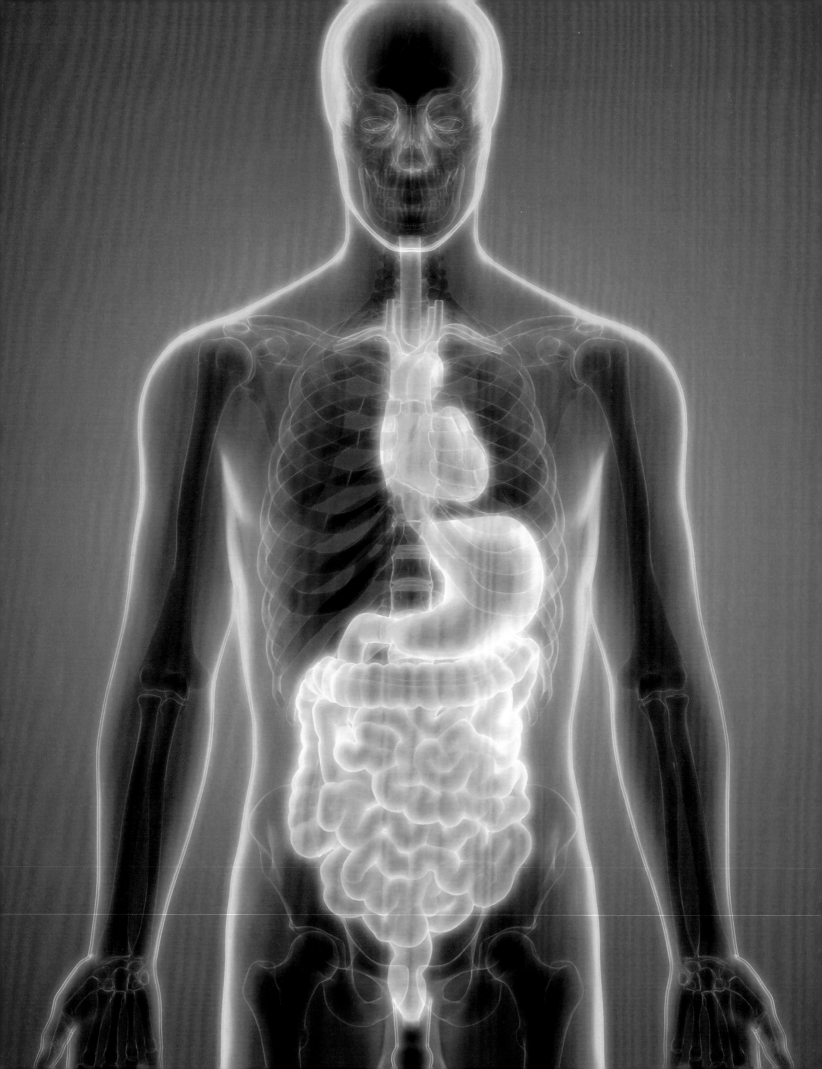

Digestive System

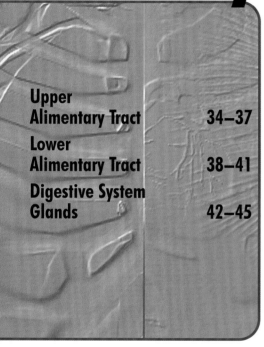

CHAPTER 4

Upper Alimentary Tract   34–37

Lower Alimentary Tract   38–41

Digestive System Glands   42–45

The function of the digestive system consists of the chemical decomposition of ingested nutrients such as fats, carbohydrates, vitamins and proteins, in a manner allowing their absorption by the intestinal capillaries. This takes place in the various sections of the digestive system, in conjunction with the numerous enzymes of the digestive glands. The nutrients are broken down in size and structure to facilitate their absorption across the mucous membranes of the gastrointestinal tract. Energy is derived from combustion of the nutrients, in order to sustain the maintenance metabolism and the associated liver functions. The energy obtained from metabolic processes is stored in organic substances and transformed into mechanical work (muscle contraction) or chemical activity (balance between extracellular and intracellular space).

The size of the energy requirement of a human organism depends on various factors. The age, weight and sex of the person will determine how much energy is needed. The type of physical work carried out by the person will naturally also play an important role. One distinguishes between the energy requirement when resting (metabolic rate at rest) and when performing physical work (working metabolic rate). Emotional reactions, mental activity or illness will also influence the energy requirement. This may be temporarily increased or decreased by these factors.

Vital for the process of digestion and the energy obtained from it is a balanced diet, essentially consisting of a nutrient combination including proteins, carbohydrates and lipids. Other important dietary components are vitamins, minerals, trace elements and of course water. The favourable effect of dietary fibre (roughage) is the peristaltic stimulation achieved.

Upper Alimentary Tract

The upper section of the digestive system consists of the oral cavity, teeth, tongue, salivary glands, pharynx and oesophagus.

Food is chopped up by the teeth (*dentes*) in the mouth, while being kneaded by the tongue and lubricated by saliva from the salivary glands.

The act of swallowing pushes the food into the oesophagus via the pharynx.

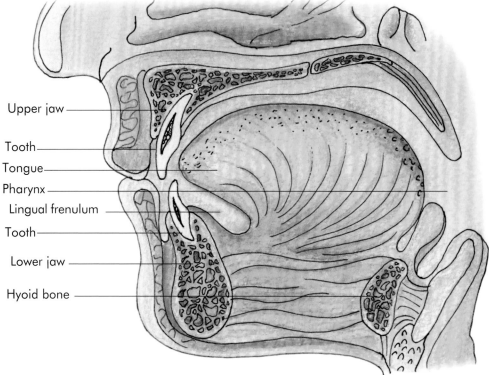

Upper jaw

Tooth

Tongue

Pharynx

Lingual frenulum

Tooth

Lower jaw

Hyoid bone

Mouth (os)

The mouth is the oral cavity, which includes the teeth and the tongue. The external edges of the mouth are formed by the lips, with the internal adjoining organ being the pharynx.

The outer skin of the lips is hairless, unpigmented and only slightly cornified. The vascular dermis shines through, resulting in the typical red colour of lips. A great number of nerves make the lips particularly sensitive to touch. Since the lips have no sweat glands, it is necessary to wet them with saliva frequently to prevent them from drying out.

The pharynx represents the connection to the openings of the digestive and respiratory systems.

The upper part of the oral cavity, the roof of the mouth, is divided into the hard palate at the front and the soft palate towards the back.

The upper jaw (maxillary bone) is located behind the hard palate.

The nasopharynx is closed off by the soft palate and velum during

Front, hard palate

Rear, soft palate

Upper lip

Teeth

Palatine velum

Uvula

Pharynx

Palatine tonsil

Tongue

Lower lip

swallowing, to prevent food from entering the respiratory tract.

The lower part of the oral cavity is formed by the lower jaw (mandible or submaxilla), on which the tongue rests. The inside of the mouth is kept moist by the mucus secreted by the oral mucosa together with the salivary gland secretions.

Teeth (dentes)

The teeth are embedded in the upper and lower jaw bones, together making up the dentition. An adult possesses 32 teeth, with 8 of them in each jaw half. The chisel-shaped incisors are located in the middle section of the superior dental arch. Together with the canine (cuspid) teeth, these are used for biting off food. The bumpy back teeth (molars or multicuspid teeth) are used for grinding pieces of food. The general formula: 2–1–2–3 means that the sequence of teeth in each jaw half starting from the inside is: 2 incisors, 1 canine, 2 premolars (bicuspids) and 3 molars.

The milk (primary or deciduous) teeth of a child consist of 20 teeth, with 2 milk incisors, 1 milk canine and 2 milk molars in each jaw half. They generally fall out at the age of seven and are replaced by a permanent dentition. The number of teeth is adapted to the size of the jaw bone.

Each tooth is divided into a root and a crown. The root of the tooth is embedded in the jaw, while the crown protrudes from the gums. Located between the root and the crown is the neck of the tooth. The hollow space within the tooth contains the tooth pulp or endodontium (blood vessels, nerve and connective tissue).

The teeth are composed of a bone-like substance, dentine *(dentinum)*. The dentine of the crown region is covered with dental enamel (adamantine substance). This is a calciferous substance, 99 % of which is crystalline, representing the hardest material in the human body.

The root of the tooth is enclosed by dental cement, a coarse-fibred bone, with the function of anchoring the tooth in the jaw. The jaw bones are covered by the oral mucosa, which protect the root of the tooth from bacteria.

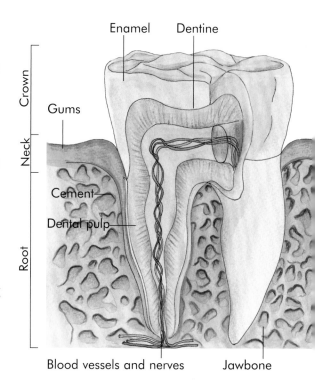

Enamel   Dentine
Crown
Gums
Neck
Cement
Dental pulp
Root
Blood vessels and nerves   Jawbone

Cross-Section of the Tongue

Vallate papilla   Covering cells of the lingual mucosa   Filiform papilla

Fossa of vallate papilla

Mucous glands   Taste buds   Connective tissue   Fungiform papilla

Tongue *(lingua)*

The rear part of the tongue is joined to the lower jaw and the hyoid (lingual) bone, and the side parts to the pharyngeal wall. It has a pointed end towards the front. The front part of the tongue is freely mobile and touches the front teeth. The underside of the tongue is attached to the lower oral cavity by means of the lingual frenulum *(frenulum linguae)*.

The tongue contains muscle fibres, responsible for its motility. The muscles from the neck and lower jaw connecting to the tongue further enhance its flexibility. The ability to shift food back and forth during chewing (mastication) with the tongue is of great significance for digestion.

Taste buds in variously shaped lingual (or gustatory) papillae (vallate, foliate and fungiform) are located on the dorsum of the tongue. The filiform papillae situated in the front region of the tongue fulfil a tactile function.

Salivary Glands of the Mouth

Three pairs of large salivary glands lead into the oral cavity:
- **Sublingual gland**
  (*glandula sublingualis*)
- **Submandibular gland**
  (*glandula submandibularis*)
- **Parotid gland**
  (*glandula parotidea*)

These are secretory *(exocrine)* glands, meaning that they secrete saliva via special excretory ducts. Small salivary glands are also located in the mucous membrane covering the cheeks, tongue, palate and inner lips.

About 1.7 litres of saliva enter the mouth every day. Saliva is composed of mucus and water. Also present in the saliva is amylase, a digestive enzyme initiating carbohydrate digestion.

Other enzymes having an antibacterial effect are also actively involved in oral hygiene.

The enzyme lysozyme is of particular relevance in this respect.

The primary function of saliva is the preparation of food for the swallowing process. It keeps the oral cavity moist, soaks the food and makes it mushy. Salivary action on the food is necessary for allowing it to be actually tasted, since the taste buds of the tongue only react to liquid substances.

Saliva composition depends on the composition of the food. Dry food induces a greater flow of saliva than fluid food. Salivation is controlled by the autonomous nervous system. Small portions of saliva are secreted continuously over 24 hours. Production of saliva is increased or decreased in response to particular stimuli. Just the thought of certain types of

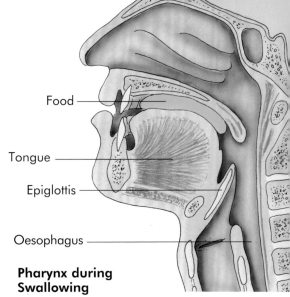

Pharynx during Swallowing

Food

Tongue

Epiglottis

Oesophagus

food (e.g. lemon) can elicit greater salivation.

Position, size and differences in tissue structure of the salivary glands result in the secretion of saliva of varying composition. Most of the **parotid gland** is located on the masseter muscle in front of the ear. It weighs 20–30 g and is normally soft and not palpable. Inflammation of the gland will cause it to swell and become hard. The viral infection, mumps *(epidemic parotiditis)* is a well-known illness.

The excretory duct of the parotid gland *(ductus parotideus)* enters the oral cavity opposite the 2nd molar.

Chewing action squeezes some of the saliva out of the gland. Despite the parotid gland being the largest salivary gland, it only produces one quarter of the daily quantity of saliva.

The **submandibular salivary gland** is located on the floor of the mouth on the inner lower jaw bone beneath the molars. It weighs 10–15 g. Its excretory duct leads to the end of the lingual frenulum and also emerges there.

The **sublingual salivary gland** weighing only 5 g, is situated below the tongue on the floor of the mouth. It is composed of a number of subglands with short excretory ducts, facilitating the transport of thick mucus.

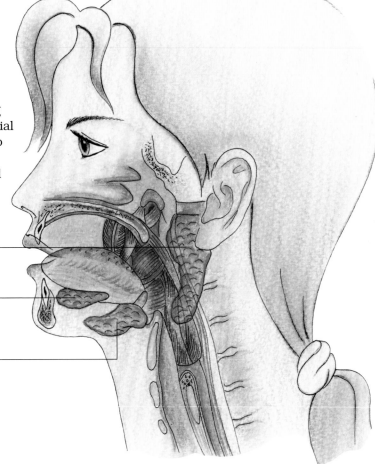

Parotid gland

Sublingual gland

Submandibular gland

Salivary Glands of the Mouth

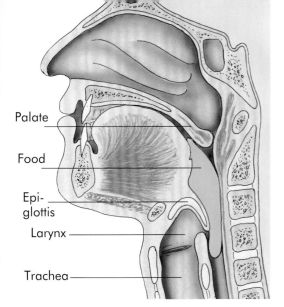

Palate

Food

Epi-
glottis

Larynx

Trachea

The epiglottis moves downwards and closes off the windpipe during food ingestion.

Pharynx

The upper part of the pharynx (see the chapter 'Respiratory System') is involved in the respiratory process, while the middle and lower pharyngeal sections play a role both in the respiratory and digestive processes.

The pharyngeal wall consists primarily of a mucous membrane and a muscular layer. The muscle layer forms the pharyngeal constrictor, divided into the superior, middle and inferior pharyngeal constrictors. These narrow the pharynx when they contract.

The food morsel slips into the back part of the oral cavity during swallowing, the food pulp (chyme) getting pushed towards the pharyngeal passages by lifting the tip of the tongue to the roof of the mouth. This stage of swallowing is voluntary and can be interrupted at will. The next stage is involuntary, controlled by the swallowing centre in the medulla oblongata. The muscles of the tongue, palate, pharynx and hyoid bone are stimulated. The larynx is lifted up and covered by the base of the tongue, while the morsel is pushed into the pharynx. In parallel, the nasopharyngeal area is closed off by the palatine velum. The food is transported from the pharynx to the oesophagus.

Gullet *(oesophagus)*

The gullet *(oesophagus)* is a tube about 25 cm in length and 1–2 cm in diameter.

The upper part of the oesophagus, the neck part *(pars cervicalis)*, is located behind the windpipe (trachea). This continues into the middle section (pars thoracica), then leading to the lower section *(pars abdominalis)*, where it is located in front of the aorta, then passing through an opening within the diaphragm, before terminating in the stomach.

The structure of the oesophagus is made up of the following four consecutive layers, starting from the inside: an inner mucous membrane, a connective tissue layer, a muscular layer and an all-enclosing connective tissue layer.

The mucosa makes food transport easier. The outer muscular layer is composed of non-striated muscle tissue, while the inner layer is constituted of a ring-shaped arrangement of fibres.

Once a morsel of food from the pharynx reaches the oesophagus, the fibres of these circular muscles contract immediately behind the food, resulting in its being pushed downwards. The food now reaches an area where the muscles are still relaxed. The previously contracted circular muscles relax again, while those now situated behind the food contract. This wave-like movement of the muscular layer is called peristalsis. This is the fastest way for the ingested food to be transported to the stomach.

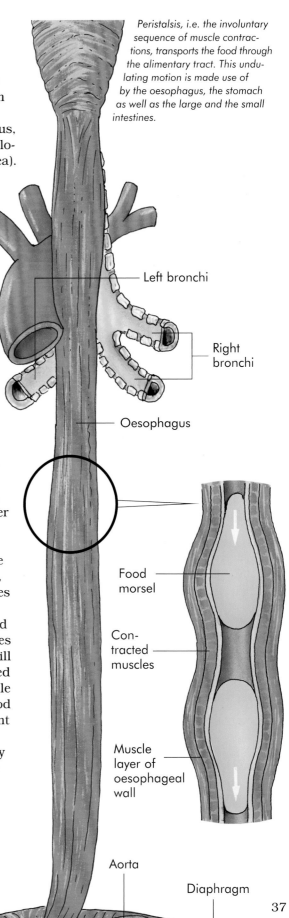

Peristalsis, i.e. the involuntary sequence of muscle contractions, transports the food through the alimentary tract. This undulating motion is made use of by the oesophagus, the stomach as well as the large and the small intestines.

Left bronchi

Right bronchi

Oesophagus

Food morsel

Contracted muscles

Muscle layer of oesophageal wall

Stomach

Aorta

Diaphragm

Lower Alimentary Tract

The lower alimentary tract is composed of the stomach, intestines and the glands of the digestive system, i.e. the liver, the gall bladder and the pancreas.

The peristaltic movement of the oesophagus transports the food to the stomach. Gastric juices are produced by the glands in the stomach lining (gastric mucous membrane) and secreted for the purpose of decomposition of the food. The chyme is mixed by means of stomach movements and transferred to the duodenum in portions via the pylorus. Bile and other enzymes for degradation are transferred to the duodenum via the common bile duct *(ductus choledochus)* and the pancreatic duct.

After several chemical processes, the chyme reaches the upper *(jejunum)* and lower *(ileum)* part of the small intestine, where final chemical degradation of the food occurs. Water is removed from the chyme in the adjoining large intestine. After passage through the sections of the large intestine, it finally reaches the rectum, where indigestible remnants are collected and excreted as faeces via the anus.

Nutrients contained in the food reach the villi of the small intestine, from where they are passed into the blood via lymph vessels, arteries, veins and capillaries.

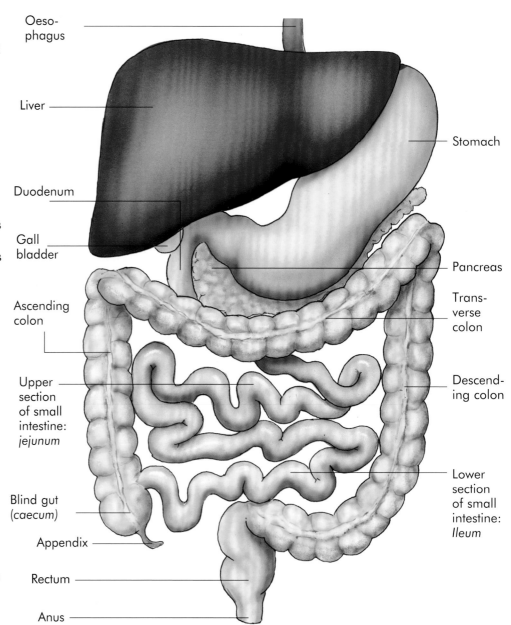

Oeso-phagus

Liver

Duodenum

Gall bladder

Ascending colon

Upper section of small intestine: *jejunum*

Blind gut *(caecum)*

Appendix

Rectum

Anus

Stomach

Pancreas

Trans-verse colon

Descend-ing colon

Lower section of small intestine: *Ileum*

Stomach *(ventriculus, Gaster)*

The stomach looks like a bent pouch. It is located in the upper left abdominal region, bordering on the liver, spleen, pancreas, diaphragm and the transverse colon. The stomach adapts its shape according to its contents and the position of the body. Different shapes may therefore be distinguished, such as hook-shaped, bugle-shaped or horn-shaped.

The oesophagus enters the stomach at the cardia *(pars cardiaca)*. The gastric fornix *(fundus gastricus)* forms an arch over the stomach.

Swallowed gases are collected here. The body of the stomach *(corpus gastricum)* curves downwards to the right, ending in the gastric outlet (pylorus). The different parts of the stomach merge without any distinctive borders.

The inside of the stomach is covered by a thick mucous membrane,

Stomach Wall Cross Section

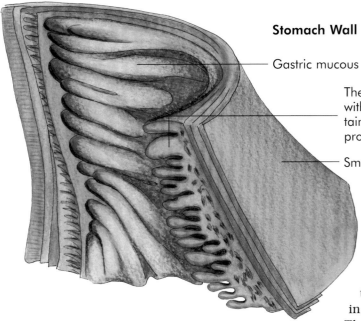

Gastric mucous membrane

The inner epithelial layer with its many folds contains mucus- and enzyme-producing cells

Smooth outer wall

in which the gastric glands are embedded.

The muscular layer of the stomach is composed of striated and non-striated muscle tissue, allowing the stomach to contract and expand, thereby continuing the peristaltic movements of the oesophagus used for transporting the food. The stomach is surrounded by the peritoneum, which facilitates slight displacement of the stomach as required by its increasing or decreasing size during food ingestion.

The gastric glands secrete various substances, depending on the cell type. The peptic cells secrete pepsinogen, which is converted to the enzyme pepsin in the stomach. It breaks down proteins (proteolysis). The parietal cells produce gastric acid (hydrochloric acid). The mucus secreted by the mucous neck cells is very important because this mucus layer protects the stomach from digesting itself.

The hormone gastrin is released by the G cells that are chiefly located in the pyloric region of the stomach. The gastrin transported by the blood to the glands of the gastric fornix and the gastric body stimulates these glands to secrete gastric juices. Gastrin continues

to be produced as long as protein-containing food arrives in the pyloric region.

The secretion of gastric juices is controlled by the sight and smell of food via the 10th cranial nerve. This neural phase represents a kind of ignition for glandular secretion, continuing with gastrin production in the hormonal phase. The preparation and order of presentation of food is therefore not insignificant for the processes taking place in the stomach. The typical menu sequence of soup – main

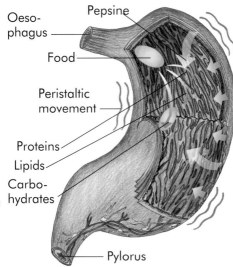

Oesophagus

Pepsine

Food

Peristaltic movement

Proteins

Lipids

Carbohydrates

Pylorus

Food enters the stomach from the oesophagus via the cardia region of the stomach. The food is mixed with the gastric juices secreted by the gastric mucous membrane. The hydrochloric acid contained in the gastric juices has an antibacterial action and activates the protein-digesting enzyme pepsin. The food pulp then passes into the small intestine via the pyloric opening.

course – dessert, is certainly an appropriate arrangement.

The chyme from the oesophagus is collected in the stomach. A meal remains in the stomach for about 3–4 hours on average. This period may be extended to about 7 hours and more for food with a very high fat content. Only such amounts of chyme as can be processed by the stomach are transferred into the duodenum.

Intestines *(intestinum)*

The major intestinal components are the small intestine *(intestinum tenue)* and the large intestine *(intestinum crassum)*.

The small intestine includes:
- **Duodenum**
- **Jejenum** (empty intestine)
- **Ileum** (twisted intestine)

The large intestine includes:
- **Caecum** (blind gut) with **Vermiform appendage** (*appendix*)
- **Colon**
- **Rectum** (straight intestine)

Similar to the stomach wall, the intestinal wall also consists of peritoneum, muscular layer and mucous membrane. The major part of the digestive process takes place in the small intestine. The intestinal wall produces enzymes for breaking down the food into small units that can be used by the body. Bile from the liver and pancreatic juices from the pancreas are also added.

Carbohydrates are decomposed in several steps to obtain simple sugars such as glucose. Proteins are split up into amino acids. The conversion of lipids into fatty acids occurs by the bile splitting the lipids into small fat droplets, in order to provide a larger surface area for attack by fat-splitting enzymes *(lipase)*.

Intestinal Cross-Section

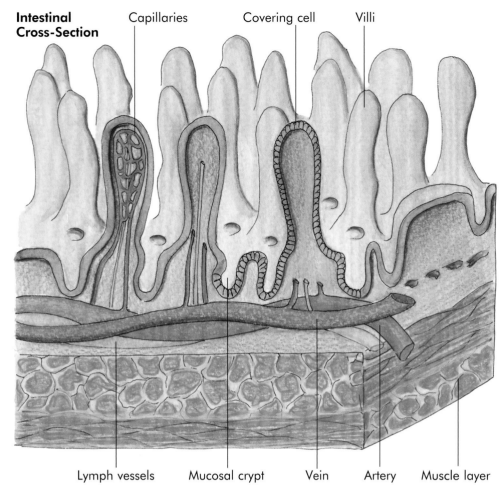

Capillaries · Covering cell · Villi

Lymph vessels · Mucosal crypt · Vein · Artery · Muscle layer

in the rectum until excretion. Food components that cannot be broken down by the digestive enzymes are referred to as dietary fibre. They are of significance for the transportation of the chyme. By increasing the volume of the chyme and thereby filling the digestive tract, this material stimulates the alimentary canal and counteracts constipation.

The surface area of the **intestinal mucosa** is greatly enlarged by finger-like projections, the intestinal villi. They are lined with numerous small vessels. The villi protrude into the chyme and absorb the digested substances, which then are transported away via the blood and lymph vessels. There is also a small contractible muscle in each villus. This villous pump accelerates the removal of digested substances.

In addition to the projections of the villi (evaginations), there are also invaginations (intestinal crypts), in which secretory cells are embedded. These secrete mucus or digestive juices.

Four cell types can be found in the intestinal mucosa.

Enterocytes (or absorbing epithelial cells) are chiefly involved

The substances derived by means of digestion that can be utilised by the body are taken up by the blood (glucose, amino acids, salts, vitamins) and the lymph (glycerol, fatty acid) and are transported to the body cells. There they are either processed immediately or stored.

Digestion is completed in the **large intestine.** In contrast to the small intestine, the large intestine is populated by a large number of bacteria (e.g. coliform bacteria). These feed on undigested food residues, particularly cellulose, which is split into sugar. The digestive juices contain a lot of water, the majority of which is withdrawn from the chyme in the large intestine and returned to the blood.

Substances that the body cannot use are converted to faeces in the large intestine, which is collected

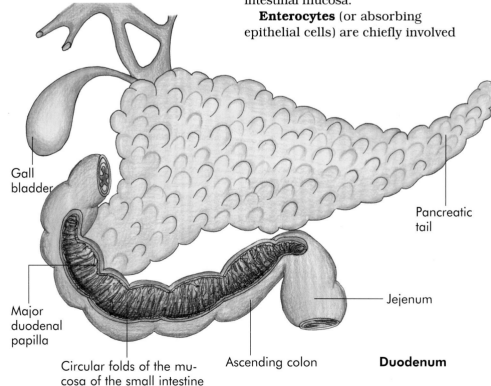

Gall bladder

Major duodenal papilla

Circular folds of the mucosa of the small intestine

Ascending colon

Pancreatic tail

Jejenum

Duodenum

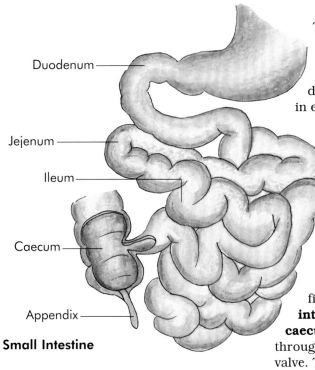

Small Intestine

in the absorption of substances. Similar to the intestinal villi, these also form small outpockets, microvilli about 1 μm in length. They lie very close to each other and form a brush border.

Goblet cells secrete mucus, while **granule cells** secrete enzymes.

The **hormonogenic cells** are part of the endocrine system. They secrete hormones that either control the work of the intestine itself or the work of specific glands or metabolic processes:

- Enterogastrone (or gastric inhibitory polypeptide, GIP) inhibits the production of gastric juices and delays emptying of the stomach.
- Secretin inhibits hydrochloric acid production in the stomach and influences the secretion of bile.
- Pancreozymin (or cholecystokinin, CCK) stimulates the production of pancreatic juices and bile secretion.
- Enterokinase increases the secretion of intestinal juices.

The **duodenum** is the first section of the small intestine, following the pylorus. It is about 30 cm (12 finger breadths) long and is C-shaped.

The common bile duct *(choledochus)* and the pancreatic duct normally enter the duodenum together; the ducts however run separately in every third person.

The following sections of the small intestine vary in length. Guideline values are 120 cm for the **jejenum** and 180 cm, for the **ileum.** The jejenum and the ileum merge without any visible borders and are not distinguishable externally.

The jejenum joins the first section of the **large intestine**, the blind gut or **caecum**. The chyme is conducted through the ileocecal (Bauhin's) valve. This allows the passage of the intestinal contents from the ileum to the caecum. A return flow is impossible.

The **caecum** is about 7 cm long and ends 'blind' with the vermiform appendage *(appendix)* in the lower right abdominal region. The vermiform appendage, which is probably involved in the body's defence system, may be as long as 10 cm and contains a lot of lymph tissue. Its position and narrowness may lead to congestion of intestinal contents. This results in the inflammation referred to as appendicitis.

The **colon** surrounds the jejenum and the ileum with an ascending part *(colon ascendens)*, a transverse part *(colon transversum)*, a descending part *(colon descendens)* and an S-shaped part *(colon sigmoideum)*. The bends in the left and right upper abdominal region are called the left and right colic flexures.

The **rectum** is also S-shaped; continuing on

from the colon, it leads to the exterior of the body with its other end, the anus. It is the final section of the large intestine. The intestinal wall is similar to that of the other sections of the intestine, apart from being particularly distensible. This ability is an important feature for the collection of faeces. The mucous membrane of the rectum possesses mucus-secreting glands. A lubricating effect is achieved by mixing the mucus with the faeces. Faeces can be excreted by contraction of the rectal muscle wall and relaxation of the sphincter muscle of the anus. Abdominal pressure, i.e. a tightening of the abdominal muscles, is used to increase the pressure.

The excrement, also referred to as stool or faeces, contains the indigestible leftovers of the food ingested and up to 75 % water. Bile pigments are responsible for the brown colour of faeces. The faecal smell is caused by the activity of the bacteria in the large intestine, also resulting in the production of gases.

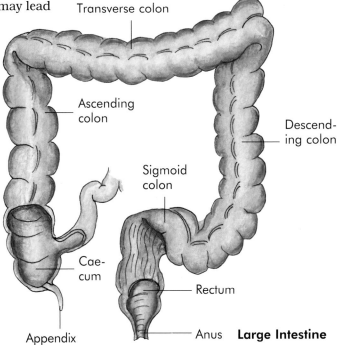

Large Intestine

41

Digestive System Glands

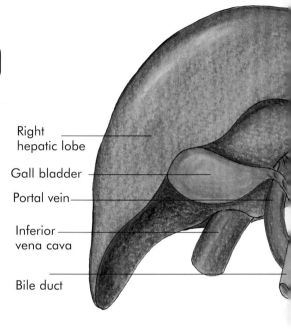

Right hepatic lobe

Gall bladder

Portal vein

Inferior vena cava

Bile duct

The organs of the digestive system responsible for producing secretions include: the liver, the gall bladder and the pancreas.

The work of the liver consists mainly of processing the basic vital substances in the food obtained by the body. These include carbohydrates, proteins and lipids. Proteins are important for growth, cell renewal and the production of enzymes and hormones. Proteins are broken down in the liver and converted into bodily structures. This process takes place in the liver cells. Carbohydrates are converted into energy. These occur chiefly in sugar-containing food.

The liver converts the various types of sugar to glucose for immediate generation of energy and to glycogen for storage. The liver converts fats into endogenous fat for storage purposes. Fats are also energy providers.

In addition to the processing, storage and release of chemical substances, the liver is also responsible for the breakdown of toxic substances and waste products. This is carried out by decomposition or neutralisation in the liver cells.

Blood breakdown products are excreted with bile formed in the liver cells. After its production, the bile is released to numerous bile canaliculi, which together form the hepatic duct. The bile is stored in the gall bladder and released, when required, into the duodenum via the bile duct, which is a continuation of the hepatic duct.

The pancreas is actually made up of two glandular systems: an endocrine (or ductless) part releasing, as the most important hormones, insulin and glucagon directly into the blood; and an exocrine part releasing the digestive enzymes produced in the pancreas into the duodenum via a duct system.

Liver (hepar)

The liver is the body's largest gland, weighing 1.4–1.8 kg in adults. It is located immediately below the diaphragm in the upper abdominal region and is completely covered by the thorax. It has a reddish brown colour. The liver is made up of a larger right hepatic lobe and a smaller left hepatic lobe. It is the 'chemical factory' of the body, responsible for a great number of tasks:

Sublingual gland

Parotid gland

Mandibular gland

Oeso-phagus

Hepatic vein

Liver

Stomach

Portal vein

Gall bladder

Duodenum

Pancreas

Small intestine

Large intestine

Rectum

*Our **digestive system** starts in the mouth and ends at the anus. The chemical breakdown of food commences in the oral cavity, where salivary enzymes (amylase) initiate carbohydrate splitting. The act of swallowing transports the food to the stomach via the oesophagus, followed by the small and then large intestines. Numerous chemical reactions take place en route, in the course of which lipids are converted to glycerol and fatty acids, to be either converted to endogenous (body's own) fats in the liver or stored as subcutaneous fat.*

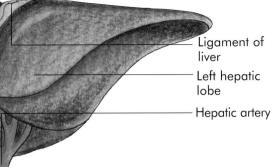

Ligament of
liver

Left hepatic
lobe

Hepatic artery

*The **liver** fulfils important functions associated with the metabolism of proteins, fats and carbohydrates as well as with detoxification. It is supplied with blood rich in nutrients by the hepatic artery from the blood circulation, as well as by the portal circulation. This allows the liver cells to be supplied with nutrient-rich blood coming straight from the digestive tract.*

• **Protein Metabolism:** The proteins ingested with food are broken down into substances usable by the body and converted to blood protein in the liver. Used-up blood protein is degraded to urea.

• **Carbohydrate Metabolism:** Simple sugar (monosaccharide) is converted to the complex sugar (polysaccharide) glycogen and stored in the liver. This is broken down again when needed, if the blood sugar level drops, and supplied to the body as glucose. Conversely, a high blood sugar level will lead to production and storage of glycogen, regulated by a hormonal control system.

• **Lipid Metabolism:** The fats ingested with food are transformed into the body's own fats and stored, e.g. in the hypodermal fatty tissue layer.

• **Detoxification:** The liver neutralises waste products from metabolic processes, toxic substances (e.g. alcohol) and other chemical substances (such as drugs).

• **Production of Bile:** This is required by the intestines for fat digestion.

A system of portal blood vessels intervenes in the transport of nutrient-enriched blood from the gastrointestinal tract. This prevents the blood from being distributed all over the body before reaching the liver.

Liver tissue is subdivided into very small functional units, the hepatic lobules. These are 1 mm in diameter and 1–2 mm in height. Their total number ranges from half a million to one million. The blood-supplying vessels are located on the lobule edges, while the blood-removing vessels are located in the middle. The bile produced by the liver cells flows away between the hepatic lobules and enters the bile system via the bile ducts.

The bile produced in the liver is referred to as liver bile.

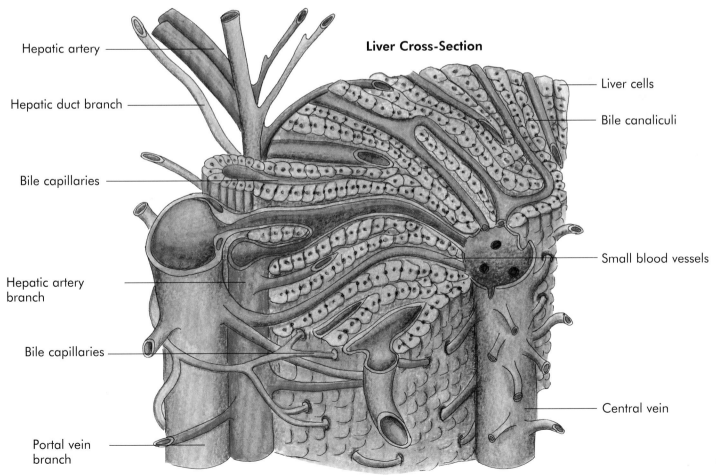

Liver Cross-Section

Hepatic artery

Hepatic duct branch

Bile capillaries

Hepatic artery
branch

Bile capillaries

Portal vein
branch

Liver cells

Bile canaliculi

Small blood vessels

Central vein

About 1 litre is produced daily. It is secreted into the gall bladder, where it is concentrated to greenish gall bladder (cystic) bile. The gall bladder is situated on the underside of the right hepatic lobe.

The bile canaliculi continue to join up to become increasingly larger bile ducts, until joining the left and right hepatic ducts and exiting from the transverse fissure *(porta hepatis)*. After uniting to become the common hepatic duct, the cystic duct (gall bladder duct) branches off to lead to the gall bladder. The hepatic duct is referred to as the (common) bile duct *(choledochus)* from then on.

If the duodenum requires bile, then it secretes the hormone cholecystokinin (CCK). As soon as this hormone reaches the gall bladder via the blood, the gall bladder contracts. The sphincter muscle of the usually common secretory duct of the bile duct and the pancreatic duct opens, and bile can flow into the duodenum.

The bile acids contained in the bile turn the lipids in the intestine into fat droplets. 80–90 % of the lipids are then returned to the liver via the blood. The degradation of red blood cells in the liver results in the haemoglobin being converted to yellowish brown bilirubin. This is responsible for the brown colour of faeces. If bile pigment enters the blood, such as after blockage of the bile duct, then the body turns yellow.

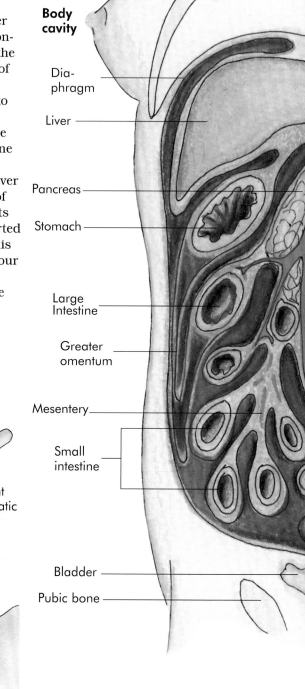

Body cavity

Diaphragm

Liver

Pancreas

Stomach

Large Intestine

Greater omentum

Mesentery

Small intestine

Bladder

Pubic bone

Gall Bladder
(vesica billaris)

The gall bladder is located on the underside of the right hepatic lobe *(lobus hepatis)*.

It is a pear-shaped pouch made of smooth muscle. The gall produced by the liver is stored in the gall bladder.

Since the capacity of the gall bladder is limited (approx 100 ml), water is withdrawn from the bile in order to keep its volume small.

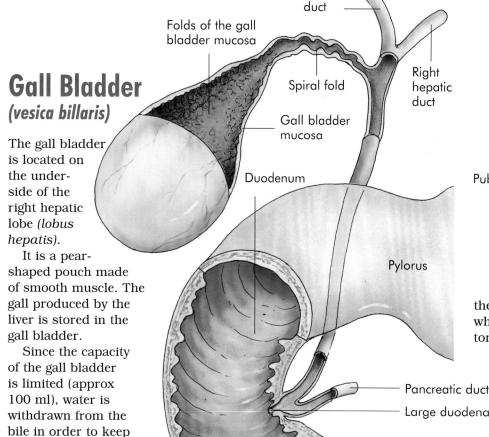

Left hepatic duct

Folds of the gall bladder mucosa

Spiral fold

Right hepatic duct

Gall bladder mucosa

Duodenum

Pylorus

Pancreatic duct

Large duodenal papilla

Bile reaches the duodenum via the cystic duct *(ductus cysticus)*, which also unites with the excretory duct of the pancreas.

Pancreas

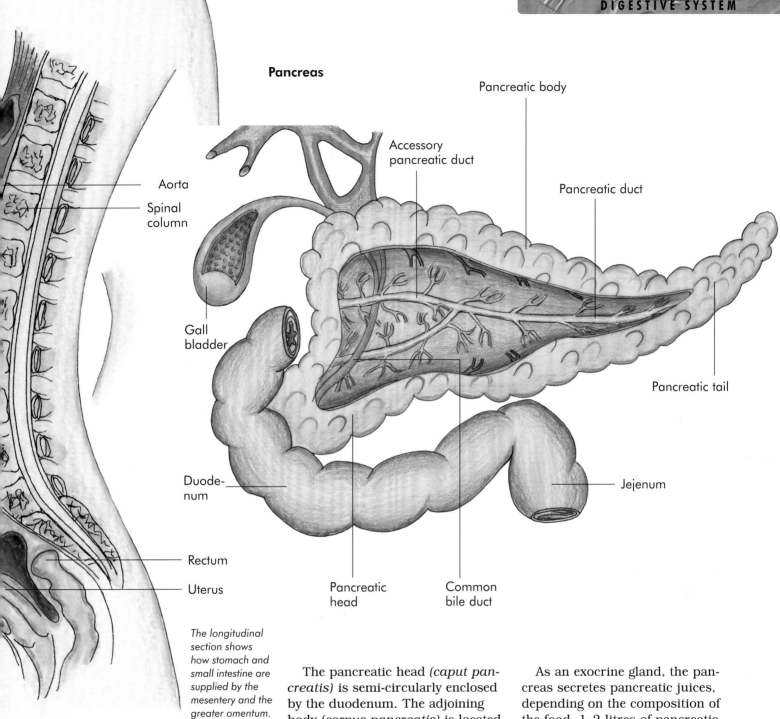

Aorta

Spinal column

Accessory pancreatic duct

Pancreatic body

Pancreatic duct

Gall bladder

Pancreatic tail

Duode-num

Jejenum

Rectum

Uterus

Pancreatic head

Common bile duct

The longitudinal section shows how stomach and small intestine are supplied by the mesentery and the greater omentum.

Pancreas

The pancreas lies across the upper abdominal (epigastric) region behind the stomach located at the height of the second lumbar vertebra. The front surface is covered by the peritoneum. It is 15–20 cm long and weighs about 80–90 g.

The pancreatic head *(caput pancreatis)* is semi-circularly enclosed by the duodenum. The adjoining body *(corpus pancreatis)* is located in front of the spinal column and aorta/inferior vena cava. The pancreatic tail *(cauda pancreatis)* reaches the spleen and upper pole of the left kidney.

The pancreas consists of secretory cells forming lobules *(acini)* that lead into small excretory ducts. These unite to form the principal excretory duct *(ductus pancreaticus)*. This flows into the duodenum together with the common bile duct.

As an exocrine gland, the pancreas secretes pancreatic juices, depending on the composition of the food. 1–2 litres of pancreatic juices are secreted every day. Gastric acid is neutralised by the bicarbonate ions contained in the juices.

The digestive enzymes produced in the pancreatic juices break down proteins and participate in carbohydrate and fat digestion. An inactive precursor form of these enzymes is stored in the pancreas; their actual activation takes place in the duodenum.

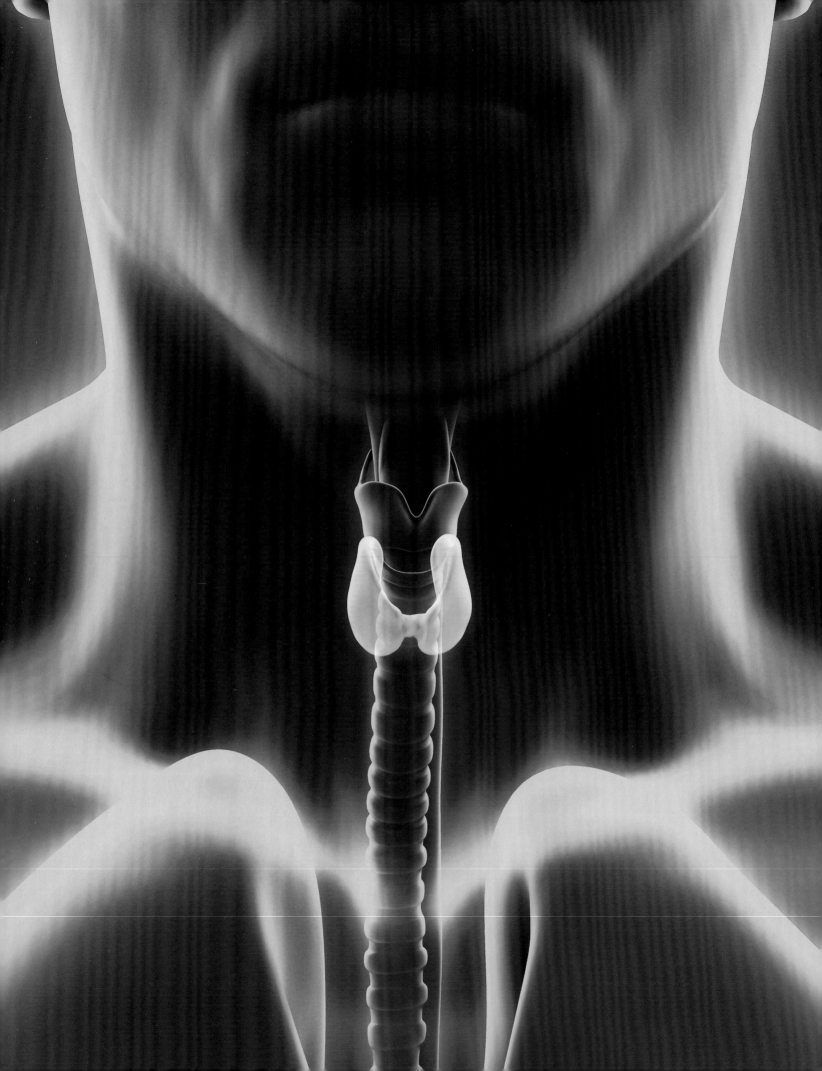

Endocrine
System

Thyroid Gland	48
Parathyroid Glands	49
Adrenal Glands	50–51
Pancreas	51
Genital Glands	52
Pituitary Gland	53
Pineal Gland	53
Endocrine Tissue	53

The activity of cells and organs in the body is coordinated by a regulatory system, the endosecretory (endocrine) system, composed of the endocrine glands and cell groups. The hormones enter the bloodstream directly, without any separate excretory ducts ('ductless'). A special control mechanism ensures 'hormonal balance'.

Each hormone has a certain sphere of activity and carries out its regulatory function by intervening in the body's metabolic processes. The hormone insulin, for instance, influences the sugar balance of the body. Each hormone has specific target cells in the organs/tissues. The hormone only becomes active when these cells recognise 'their' hormone. The quantity of hormones released is in the milligram range, often merely a fraction thereof.

The hypothalamus coordinates hormone production by the endocrine glands. This is carried out by means of so-called releasing hormones produced in the hypothalamus, which in turn stimulate the hypophysis, or pituitary gland, to secrete pituitary hormones. Once these reach the hormone glands in the body, the glands respond by producing their specific hormones. Inhibitory and activating impulses of the hormones released into the blood are fed back to the pituitary and the hypothalamus. The thyroid, adrenal glands and gonads are controlled in this manner. The production and secretion of hormones by other endocrine glands and cell groups are controlled by modification of metabolic parameters.

Hormone glands in the strict sense are the pituitary, parathyroid and adrenal glands. Glands fulfilling functions additional to hormone production are the pancreas and gonads (testicle, ovary).

Cells or cell groups producing tissue hormones are located in the stomach, intestines, kidneys and interbrain.

Thyroid Gland *(glandula thyreoidea)*

The two oval lateral lobes *(lobus dexter, lobus sinister)* of the thyroid gland are located to the right and left side of the trachea, below the larynx.

The two lobes are connected to each other by means of a narrow tissue bridge, the isthmus, located at the height of the 2nd–4th tracheal cartilage.

The gland is surrounded by a connective tissue capsule. It weighs 18–60 g and is normally soft with a brown to bluish red colour. Like all endocrine glands, it is well-perfused with blood. Changes such as hardening and significant enlargement (goitre, *struma*) are not uncommon and may indicate malfunction.

Vesicles (thyroid follicles) are recognisable by the fact that they are covered with a simple epithelium (epithelial tissue). Number, structure and size of the follicles vary according to the functional condition.

A less active thyroid is characterised by a flat to cuboidal epithelium. The epithelium increases in height with increasing activity and becomes columnar.

The thyroid hormones triiodothyronine (T3) and thyroxine (T4) are responsible for energy turnover in the body. Iodine, which is taken up from food, is required for their production. An appropriate supply of hormones is necessary for optimal maintenance of metabolic reactions.

Hypofunction *(hypothyroidism)* or hyperfunction *(hyperthyroidism)* of the thyroid are therefore expressed by morphological changes and influences on the energy turnover of the body. Reduced secretion of T3 and T4 results in a decrease in the combustion processes taking place in the body.

Physical and mental performance is restricted, body weight increases in spite of a lack of appetite, and feeling chilly is frequently reported. A hard type of struma (goitre, thyrocele) may be formed if the hypofunction persists over a longer period of time.

Increased hormone secretion results in affected persons losing weight due to stepped-up metabolism; they become more irritable and physical performance drops. A soft type of struma develops. Calcitonin, a further thyroid hormone, reduces the blood calcium level.

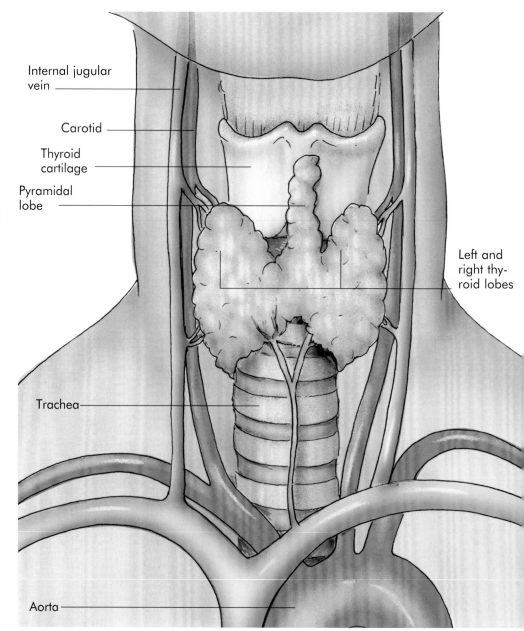

Internal jugular vein

Carotid

Thyroid cartilage

Pyramidal lobe

Left and right thyroid lobes

Trachea

Aorta

Parathyroid Glands *(glandulae parathyreoideae)*

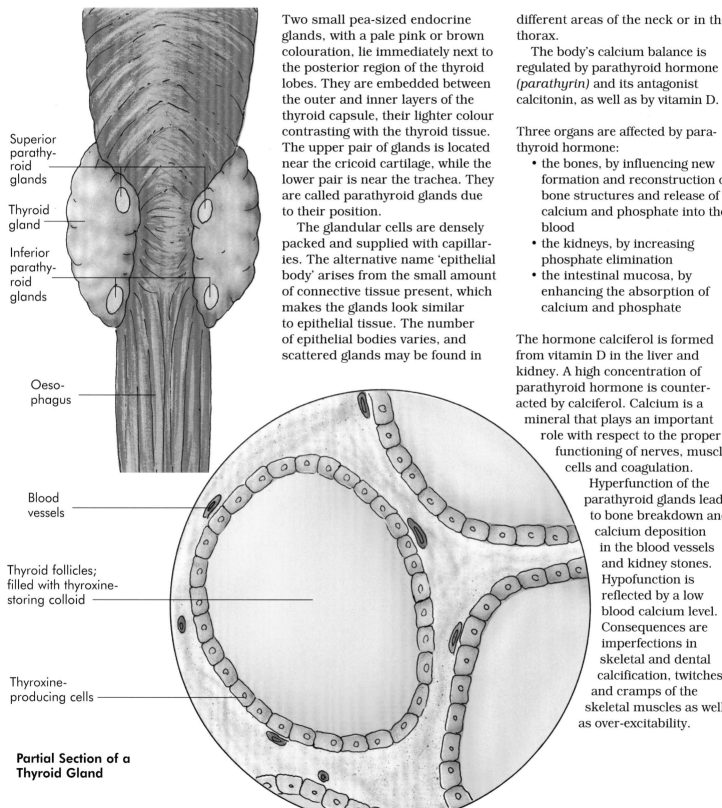

Superior parathyroid glands

Thyroid gland

Inferior parathyroid glands

Oesophagus

Blood vessels

Thyroid follicles; filled with thyroxine-storing colloid

Thyroxine-producing cells

Partial Section of a Thyroid Gland

Two small pea-sized endocrine glands, with a pale pink or brown colouration, lie immediately next to the posterior region of the thyroid lobes. They are embedded between the outer and inner layers of the thyroid capsule, their lighter colour contrasting with the thyroid tissue. The upper pair of glands is located near the cricoid cartilage, while the lower pair is near the trachea. They are called parathyroid glands due to their position.

The glandular cells are densely packed and supplied with capillaries. The alternative name 'epithelial body' arises from the small amount of connective tissue present, which makes the glands look similar to epithelial tissue. The number of epithelial bodies varies, and scattered glands may be found in different areas of the neck or in the thorax.

The body's calcium balance is regulated by parathyroid hormone *(parathyrin)* and its antagonist calcitonin, as well as by vitamin D.

Three organs are affected by parathyroid hormone:
- the bones, by influencing new formation and reconstruction of bone structures and release of calcium and phosphate into the blood
- the kidneys, by increasing phosphate elimination
- the intestinal mucosa, by enhancing the absorption of calcium and phosphate

The hormone calciferol is formed from vitamin D in the liver and kidney. A high concentration of parathyroid hormone is counteracted by calciferol. Calcium is a mineral that plays an important role with respect to the proper functioning of nerves, muscle cells and coagulation. Hyperfunction of the parathyroid glands leads to bone breakdown and calcium deposition in the blood vessels and kidney stones. Hypofunction is reflected by a low blood calcium level. Consequences are imperfections in skeletal and dental calcification, twitches and cramps of the skeletal muscles as well as over-excitability.

Adrenal Glands *(glandulae suprarenales)*

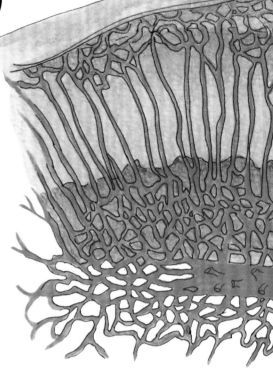

Each of the two adrenal (or supra-renal) glands is located on the respective upper kidney pole, separated by a thin lipid layer. When viewed from the front, the left adrenal gland is crescent-shaped, while the right gland is triangular. The adrenal glands weigh 5–10 g and are composed of two different types of tissue, the inner adrenal medulla and the outer adrenal cortex. The adrenal cortex consists of ganglion cells and specific medullary cells.

The hormones adrenaline and noradrenaline are formed by two different types of medullary cells, and are released into the blood mainly via the capillaries. In dangerous and stressful situations, both hormones put the body into a state of action, but they deviate slightly in their effect.

Adrenaline is secreted particularly during psychological excitation: Cardiac activity increases, blood pressure rises, blood vessels constrict (pale face) and the blood sugar level rises. The body is 'ready for action'. Adrenaline secretion stops once the excitation subsides.

Three layers can be observed in the adrenal cortex. Spherical glandular complexes make up the **outer layer** of the cortex *(zona glomerulosa)*. The mineralocorticoid hormone group is produced here, with the hormone aldosterone being particularly important. It is involved in mineral metabolism, thereby also regulating the body's water balance. The release of sodium ions into the urine, saliva and perspiration is inhibited by increasing the uptake of sodium ions in the lower section of the renal tubules and other glands.

The sodium ions form salt molecules, which bind water molecules and therefore influence the water balance of the organism. This results in an increase in blood volume and in turn of the pumping performance of the heart.

Aldosterone secretion is chiefly controlled by the concentrations of sodium and potassium ions in the blood. Low sodium and high potassium ion content activates aldosterone secretion. In addition, a balanced aldosterone level in the blood is also maintained by the hormone renin, secreted by the kidneys.

Falling below the required aldosterone level in the blood will result in increased renin secretion, thereby stimulating aldosterone secretion. An aldosterone deficit leads to excessive elimination. Overproduction results in too much retention of sodium and water in the body. This leads to high blood pressure.

In the **middle layer** *(zona fasciculata)*, the largest cortical layer, the cells are arranged perpendicularly to the surface, like beams. They produce the glucocorticoid hormone group, important in carbohydrate metabolism. These include in particular the hormone cortisol and its degradation product cortisone.

Cortisol (hydrocortisone) intervenes in carbohydrate metabolism by promoting the conversion of proteins into glucose when an increased glucose demand exists. This opposes the action of insulin. Cortisol furthermore has an anti-inflammatory action and therefore plays an important role in the immune system.

Hormone production and secretion is regulated by interaction with the pituitary and the hypothalamus. This allows the development of an unspecific resistance against stress situations, i.e. an adaptation to the stress-triggered change takes place.

The middle layer breaks up in the direction of the adrenal medulla

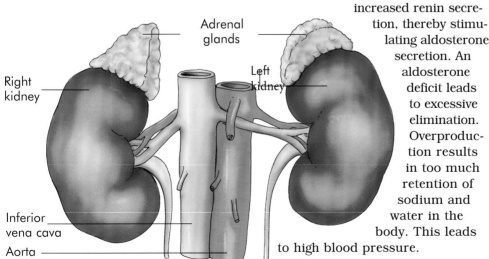

Adrenal glands

Left kidney

Right kidney

Inferior vena cava

Aorta

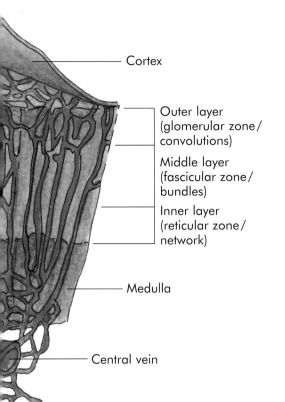

Cortex

Outer layer
(glomerular zone/
convolutions)

Middle layer
(fascicular zone/
bundles)

Inner layer
(reticular zone/
network)

Medulla

Central vein

(medulla glandulae suprarenalis) to form an irregular network of cell strands, which constitutes the inner layer *(zona reticularis)*. Both zones produce sex hormones, whose action is linked to that of the gonadal hormones. The androgens are the main group of sex hormones produced in the adrenal gland. They are responsible for the development of male sexual characteristics and occur in both men and women.

In women, the female sex hormones oestrogen and progestogen mitigate these effects. Women assume a more masculine appearance if a malfunction results in an overproduction of androgens. The decreasing production of oestrogen and progestogen during menopause can lead to the emergence of masculine physical characteristics, e.g. signs of facial hair.

The enhancing action of androgens on muscle development is taken advantage of in the disputed use of anabolic steroids (androgen derivatives). Long-term use generally leads to complications detrimental to the body.

Pancreas *(Pancreas)*

Up to 1.5 million small 'islets' of endocrine cells are embedded in the body and tail parts of the pancreas, with the pancreatic tail being most densely populated. These so-called islets of Langerhans are named after the scientist who discovered them. They are also referred to as the pancreatic islets or the endocrine part of the pancreas, due to their association with the endocrine system. The cells making up the islets of Langerhans are distinctly different from the exocrine pancreatic secretory cells.

Each of the 100–500 μm-large islets is separated from the surrounding secretory cells by connective tissue and is composed of 3,000 hormone-producing cells on average. Their blood supply is ensured by means of a capillary network. The cells of the pancreatic islets can be histochemically classified into alpha, beta and delta cells, using appropriate staining techniques.

As endocrine glands ('ductless glands'), the islets of Langerhans chiefly produce two hormones that oppose each other in their action. The hormone insulin is produced by the beta cells, which make up two thirds of the islets of Langerhans. An increase in the glucose level (dextrose) in the blood is registered after the uptake of food. Insulin is released and the cell membranes of the body cells become permeable to glucose. If the entire amount of glucose is not required by the body immediately, it is stored as glycogen (starch) in the liver and muscles. Glycogen is released again and converted to glucose once energy requirements rise.

The alpha cells are responsible for releasing the hormone glucagon into the blood whenever the blood sugar level has dropped too low. Conversion into starch is halted and stored starch is transformed back into sugar. A shortage of insulin will result in inefficient sugar combustion in the tissue, with the blood sugar level rising in consequence. The persistence of this metabolic dysfunction over a longer period of time leads to diabetes *(diabetes mellitus)*.

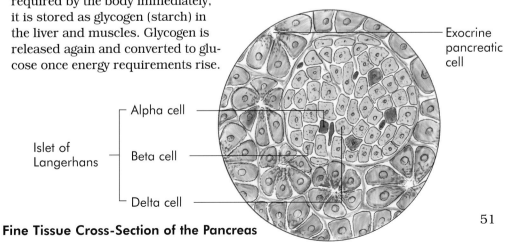

Islet of
Langerhans

Alpha cell

Beta cell

Delta cell

Exocrine
pancreatic
cell

Fine Tissue Cross-Section of the Pancreas

Genital Glands

Specific cells are responsible for the production of sex hormones and the related action of the testicles *(testis)* and ovaries *(ovarium)* as endocrine glands These are the Leydig's cells (or interstitial cells) in the testicle, and the follicular cells together with other cell complexes in the ovary.

There are male and female sex hormones, which, despite their sex-specific biological action, are required by both genders. They

Uterus

Fallopian tube

Ovarian vessels

Ovary

Fimbriae of fallopian tube

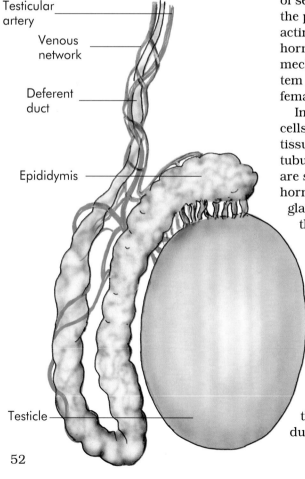

Testicular artery

Venous network

Deferent duct

Epididymis

Testicle

are therefore observed alongside each other in the male and female body. The production and secretion of sex hormones is controlled by the pituitary gland via hormones acting on the gonads (gonadotropic hormones). The complex control mechanisms of the endocrine system are particularly evident in the female cycle.

In the **testicles**, groups of Leydig's cells are embedded in connective tissue between the seminiferous tubules *(tubuli seminiferi)*. They are stimulated by the luteinizing hormone (LH) of the pituitary gland. Because of the fact that the interstitial cells are stimulated, the term interstitial cell stimulating hormone (ICSH) is also used to describe this hormone.

The male sex hormones are produced in the testicles, with quantities ranging from 2–10 mg per day. Testosterone in particular is aimed at the development of secondary sexual characteristics and the stimulation of sperm production. It also causes the growth

of the prostate gland and the seminal vesicles and maintains normal genital function.

The **ovaries** primarily produce follicular hormones *(oestrogens)*. Their functions include stimulation of the growth of the uterine mucous membrane *(endometrium)* during the menstrual cycle. Oestrogens are involved in the development of female sexual characteristics. They also participate in other metabolic processes, such as the promotion of bone formation.

Another hormone group, the progestogens *(gestagens)*, is produced in the yellow body of the ovary *(corpus luteum)* during the second half of the menstrual cycle. The principal representative, progesterone, is mainly responsible for embedding the fertilised egg in the mucosa. The placenta can be formed from this in conjunction with blastocyst tissue, in the event of a pregnancy (see section on 'Pregnancy').

The hormonal regulation of the female menstrual cycle is also characterised by a finely adjusted interplay of pituitary and sex hormones, on the basis of the feedback principle.

Pituitary Gland *(hypophysis)*

Our growth and gender-related be-haviour is controlled by the release of appropriate hormones by the pituitary gland, which is part of the endocrine system, in combination with the hypothalamus. Together with the pineal gland, it forms a sort of clock for specific rhythms associated with our lives, such as the lunar, daily and weekly rhythms.

The approximately pea-sized pituitary gland has an anterior and posterior lobe and is located near the base of the skull below the optic chiasm.

The pituitary is under the con-trol of the hypothalamus, being linked to the latter by the pituitary or hypophysial stalk. It is a mor-phological part of the interbrain (or diencephalon).

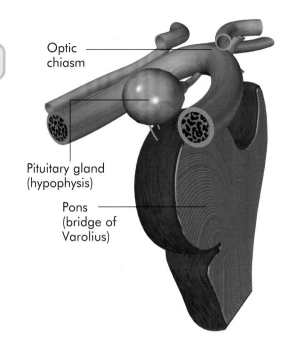

Optic chiasm

Pituitary gland (hypophysis)

Pons (bridge of Varolius)

Pineal Gland *(corpus pineale, epiphysis)*

Pituitary gland

Cere-brum

Thalamus

Pineal gland

Pons

Cerebellum

The function of the pineal gland (or pineal body) has yet to be elucidated further. Known are, for instance, its photosensitivity and its interactive function with the hypophysis (pituitary) for main-taining diverse vital processes as part of an endocrine dipole, with the hypophysis as the positive and the epiphysis as the negative pole.

The pineal gland is morphologi-cally part of the epithalamus and therefore also part of the interbrain. It is important in the coordination of hormonal processes by the hypo-thalamus. It produces melatonin, an important hormone for the develop-ment of the gonads. It was believed to be the 'seat of the soul' in earlier centuries.

Endocrine Tissue

In addition to the endocrine glands, hormone-producing cells and cell groups are distributed throughout the body. Some of the hormones produced there reach their target organs via the blood. Others act at their site of produc-tion.

An entire system of endocrine cells can be found in the gastroin-testinal tract. Their hormones stim-ulate, for example, the production of gastric juices; gastrin is dis-charged via the stomach, thereby influencing hydrochloric acid forma-tion; pancreozymin (cholecystokinin)

is produced in the duodenum for stimulation of the pancreatic en-zymes.

Hormone-producing cells secret-ing renin are also located in the kidneys. One of the effects achieved by this includes the release of aldosterone in the adrenal gland.

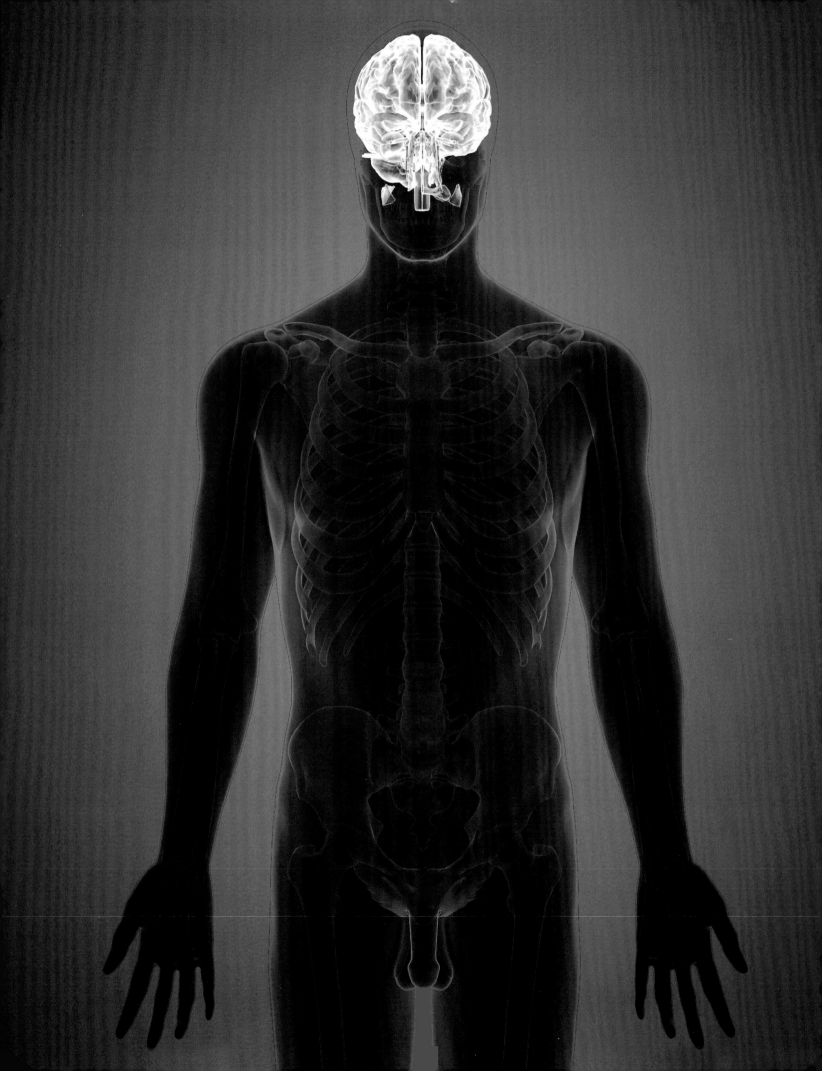

CHAPTER 6

Brain/Nervous System

Central Nervous System 56–57

Vegetative Nervous System 58

Nerves 58–61

The human nervous system links the entire body to the brain (*cerebrum*), which is its supreme centre of control. All bodily processes are regulated and coordinated appropriately by the brain. Stimuli originating from outside or inside the body are directed to the spinal cord (*medulla spinalis*) and the brain. These are processed there, and instructions concerning the response to the stimuli are sent to the tissues and organs.

The nervous system is divided into the central nervous system, including the spinal cord and brain, the peripheral nervous system, comprising all nerves connecting the central nervous system to the body periphery (e.g. sensory organs, muscles), as well as the vegetative nervous system, which includes the sympathetic and the parasympathetic nervous systems.

Central Nervous System

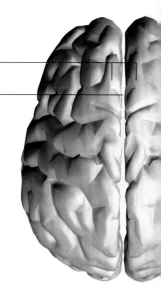

Hemispheres

Longitudinal
cerebral fissure

The brain *(cerebrum)* and the spinal cord *(medulla spinalis)* make up the central nervous system (CNS). Nerves project in bundles from this central system all the way to the nervous system periphery.

Signals from the peripheral nervous system are analysed and stored, and motor signals are produced in the CNS. This capability, which is mainly the responsibility of the brain, is very complicated, requiring the participation of innumerable nerve cells (neurocytes or neurons). The most demanding function of the nervous system is fulfilled by the cerebral cortex. This is the seat of our thinking, our will and our sensations, the centre for all bodily functions, as it were.

Our conception of our surroundings, of good and bad, of right and wrong, and of beautiful and ugly, is created in the cerebral cortex.

An extensive vascular network supplies the central nervous system with oxygen and nutrients. The CNS is embedded in cavities surrounded by bone, formed by the skull in the head region and the vertebral arches in the neck and trunk area. This provides external protection of the brain and spinal cord.

This protection is enhanced internally by three connective tissue layers.

Brain

Spinal cord

These enclose the brain in the shape of meninges (plural of meninx) in the head, while also surrounding the spinal cord in the spinal column. The gap between the middle and inner layer is filled with cerebrospinal fluid (neurolymph).

Brain *(cerebrum)*

It is the brain that distinguishes human beings decisively from other creatures. It enables us to act consciously and think logically. It is the site of central administration of our thoughts, control centre for almost every movement, seat of our feelings and emotions, equally responsible for conscious and unconscious actions.

An adult brain weighs between 1200 and 1500 g. In comparison with other creatures, human beings

This fluid provides the most extensive protection of the central nervous system from mechanical damage.

do not have the largest brain, neither absolutely (an elephant brain weighs about 5000 g), nor relatively (a sparrow beats us to it here).

The brain is composed of four major sections:
• **Cerebrum** (upper brain)
• **Brainstem** (encephalic trunk)
• **Diencephalon** (interbrain)
• **Cerebellum**

The cerebrum is the largest part of the human brain anatomically.

The cerebrum controls our conscious actions and is furthermore

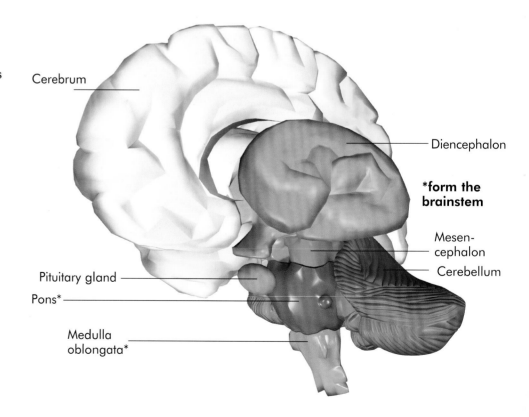

Cerebrum

Diencephalon

*form the brainstem

Mesencephalon

Cerebellum

Pituitary gland

Pons*

Medulla oblongata*

the seat of intelligence, learning and teaching ability, memory, will and feeling. The cerebellum coordinates our movements and is responsible for our sense of balance and spatial orientation. The brainstem regulates our breathing, circulation, sleeping-waking rhythm, our attentiveness,

to name but a few functions, and is directly or indirectly linked with all parts of the central nervous system.

The brain, which is part of the CNS, is protected just like the spinal cord, by means of a bony capsule (here the cranial cavity) and covered by the meninges, en-

closing the brain and containing the cushioning cerebrospinal fluid.

All-round mechanical protection is therefore provided for both the brain and spinal cord of the central nervous system, by means of a bony as well as a tissue and fluid-containing layer.

Spinal Cord
(medulla spinalis)

This part of the central nervous system is accommodated in an osseous enclosure. The neural arches of the vertebrae form a spinal canal in the neck and trunk region. The spinal cord is enclosed within. Similar to the spinal column, this is divided into four sections. A spinal nerve emerges to the left and right from each of these sections.

Nerve cells are concentrated in some areas of the spinal cord. These are called grey matter (or substance) due to their yellowish grey colour. The areas of the spinal cord in which the long nerve processes are situated are white in appearance and are therefore referred to as white matter (or substance).

The grey matter located at the core of the spinal cord is butterfly-shaped. Nerves from sensory cells lead to the grey matter. From here, some of them lead to motor nerves, while others lead to the brain via the white matter. Nerves coming from higher sections of the central nervous system first pass into the grey matter and then out of the spinal cord to the target organ.

Very specific assignment of the nerves situated in the white matter is possible, e.g. a path responsible for involuntary movements required for maintaining balance or a path

for perception of warmth and coldness. On their way from spinal cord to brain, these paths change sides, i.e. they cross or 'decussate' *(pyramidal decussation)*.

Injuries transecting the white matter of the spinal cord lead to paraplegia.

The parts of the body located below the site of injury are then no longer connected to the brain.

Very fast reactions to specific stimuli, not directly involving the cerebrum also occur via the spinal cord: these are the reflexes.

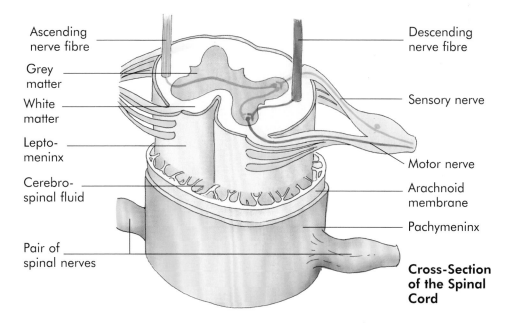

Ascending nerve fibre

Grey matter

White matter

Lepto-meninx

Cerebro-spinal fluid

Pair of spinal nerves

Descending nerve fibre

Sensory nerve

Motor nerve

Arachnoid membrane

Pachymeninx

Cross-Section of the Spinal Cord

Spinal Nerves

A total of 31 spinal nerve pairs passes through the intervertebral foramen left and right, heading towards the periphery. Their number corresponds to the number of spinal cord segments. Leading away from each side are therefore:

- **8 Cervical nerves** (*Nn. cerivicales*)
- **12 Thoracic nerves** (*Nn. thoracici*)
- **5 Lumbar nerves** (*Nn. lumbales*)
- **5 Sacral nerves** (*Nn. sacrales*)
- **1 Coccygeal nerve** (*N. coccygeus*)

Each of these nerve groups supplies certain body regions according to their location. Damage may lead to loss of function of the relevant region, e.g. due to paraplegia.

Vegetative Nervous System

The vegetative nervous system includes parts of the peripheral and central nervous systems. It controls all the involuntary processes of the lungs *(pulmo)*, heart *(cor)*, blood vessels (arteries/veins), stomach *(ventriculus)*, intestine *(intestinum)* and urinary bladder *(vesica urinari)* by means of the hypothalamus in the brain. This occurs via reflex arcs, which elicit motor impulses in the organs, initiated by impulses

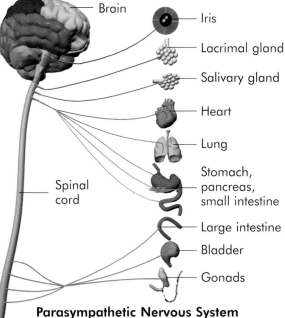

Parasympathetic Nervous System

from receptors located on the internal organs.

The vegetative nervous system is chiefly responsible for maintenance of the organism's internal conditions and for regulating organ functions if required. This is achieved by co-operation between the **sympathetic** und **parasympathetic nervous systems**.

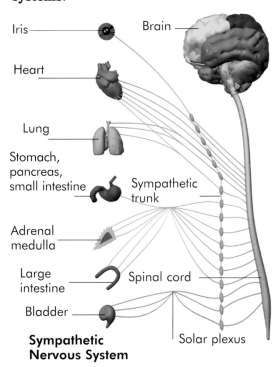

Sympathetic Nervous System

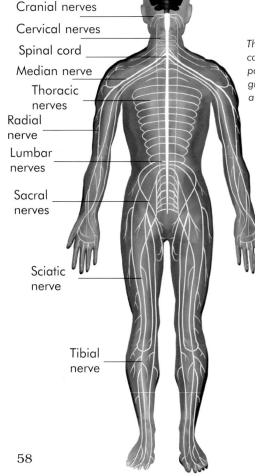

*The **peripheral nervous system** includes pathways connecting the central nervous system with all other body parts as well as with ganglia, i.e. intermediate nerve cell-groups. The peripheral nervous system is composed of a voluntarily and involuntarily controlled part.*

Nerves

In addition to the central and vegetative (autonomous) nervous systems, there is also a peripheral nervous system. Its cells connect the central nervous system to the body periphery. Their path links the brain or spinal cord directly to the muscles, skin or sensory organs. These are generally mixed nerves with sensory (receptor) fibres and motor fibres.

Sensory fibres chiefly originate in neuroganglia (spinal ganglia), connected to the spinal cord via the posterior root. Motor fibres generally leave the spinal cord via the anterior root. The diameter of nerves ranges from as thin as a hair to as thick as a rope.

Peripheral Nervous System

The peripheral nervous system is chiefly composed of nerves connecting the central nervous system with other body parts as well as with the intermediate groups of nerve cells, the ganglia. 12 nerve pairs leave the cranium as cranial nerves, while 31 nerve pairs leave the spinal cord as spinal nerves.

Similar to the blood vessels, the nerves of the peripheral nervous system lead directly from the brain or spinal cord all over the body, connecting all organs and tissues by means of a network of fine branches. The cranial nerves are primarily linked to our sensory organs and the muscles of the head.

In the abdominal and thoracic region, the spinal nerves supply the back as well as the thoracic and abdominal walls. In the neck and shoulder girdle region as well as in the lumbar and sacral regions, the spinal nerves form a network mainly supplying the limbs. Spinal nerves are always composed of motor and sensory nerve fibres (neurofibres).

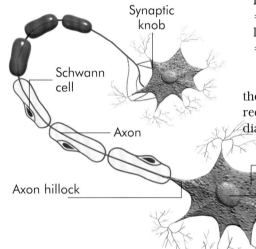

Synaptic knob

Schwann cell

Axon

Axon hillock

Cell body

Nucleus of the nerve

Dendrites

Nerve Cell *(neuron)*

Each nerve consists of a number of neurons (neurocytes), and each neuron is composed of:
• cell body (perikaryon), the
• actual nucleus (karyon) and the
• cell processes (extensions)
  leading away (efferent)
  = axons (cone-shaped)
  leading toward (afferent)
  = dendrites (branch-shaped)

Axons connect the neurons to their neighbouring cells. Dendrites receive the signals from their immediate surroundings.

Nerve Fibres

The excitation impulse of human nerve cells is conducted along the surface of the nerve cell process (dendrite or axon). This requires the insulation of each nerve cell extension from the other, achieved by enveloping them in sheaths (neurilemmal sheath). A nerve fibre is composed of a nerve cell process encased in a sheath.

Nerve fibres are differentiated as myelinated or nonmyelinated neurofibres. Myelinated nerve fibres are well-insulated. The cell body of the myelin sheath cell (Schwann cell) is wrapped around the nerve process spirally.

There is a gap in the myelin sheath at the junction of two sheath cells in the shape of a circular groove (node of Ranvier).

This allows the excitation of the nerve fibre to jump from node to node. The thicker the fibre and the larger the distances between the nodes, the faster the excitation impulse is conveyed. One distinguishes fibres on the basis of their speed of conduction: there are A fibres (20–100 m/s), B fibres (10 m/s) and C fibres (1 m/s).

Nonmyelinated nerve fibres are less well-insulated. They are often simply located in the cell body of the sheath cell together with other nerve fibres. They have neither sheath nor node. The excitation is therefore conducted much more slowly. Nonmyelinated nerve fibres are mainly found in the vegetative nervous system.

Afferent and efferent nerve fibres are distinguished, depending on the direction of conduction (toward or away). Afferent nerve fibres lead impulses from the periphery of the body towards the central nervous system (or also from lower to higher centres within the CNS). Efferent nerve fibres conduct in the opposite direction.

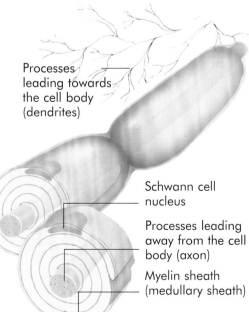

Processes leading towards the cell body (dendrites)

Schwann cell nucleus

Processes leading away from the cell body (axon)

Myelin sheath (medullary sheath)

Nerve Control
Voluntary movements are elicited by excitation of the cerebral cortex. These impulses are transmitted to the muscles via the neuronal paths of the spinal cord and the motor nerves.

Cerebral cortex

Motor nerve

Spinal cord

Nerve fibre

Muscle

Stimulus and Pain

Pain is an important part of our essential warning system.

The sensation may vary from dull to stabbing, from slight to almost unbearable.

Any kind of injury results in the acute sensation of pain being directed to the spinal cord and brain via sensory nerves. The first segment of the transmission of impulses *(neuron)* conducts the signal to the dorsal horn of the spinal cord via very fast nerve fibres. These are type A nerve fibres. A different neuron takes up the signal at this point, in order to bring it to the other side of the spinal cord, from where it is transmitted to the thalamus in the diencephalon.

Dull and longer-lasting pain is reported by a slower path via non-myelinated type C nerve fibres. The impulse is conducted through a chain of interconnected neurons, starting from the spinal cord, continuing to the brainstem, followed by the thalamus and leading finally to the cerebral cortex.

The vegetative nervous system is also capable of receiving pain signals and transmitting them to the brain. Since the internal organs supplied by the vegetative system are only equipped with few sensory receptors, exact localisation of the generally dull pain arising there is difficult.

Transmission of Impulses – In order to be perceived as pain, a stimulus has to exceed a certain measure. The pain threshold, which can also be modified under certain conditions, is determined by a fixed regulatory system.

The pain signal is transmitted by T-cells in the spinal cord. These are activated by the nerve fibres at the site of stimulation. Located in the gelatinous substance *(substantia gelatinosa)* of the dorsal horn of the spinal cord are other cells, which inhibit the T-cell impulse transmission. These are initiated by the stimuli of the larger nerve fibres on the one hand, while being slowed down by the smaller and slower type C fibres.

The fibres for touch are activated together with the cells of the substantia gelatinosa if there is no sensation of pain. This inhibits the T-cells and no pain is perceived. Incidence of pain will however cause the activity of the C fibres to increase until the inhibitory threshold of the large fibres to the substantia gelatinosa is overcome. This allows the

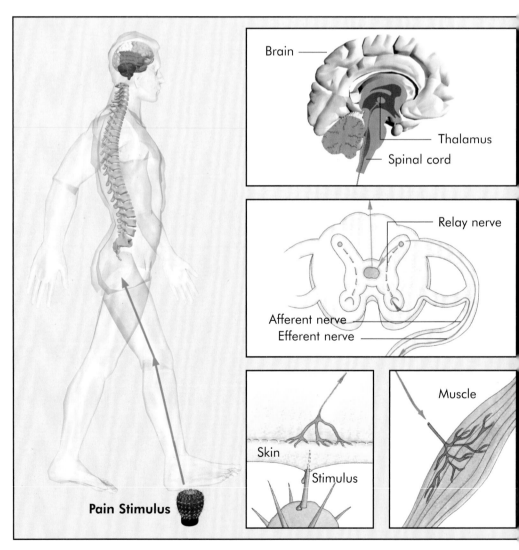

Pain Stimulus

Brain

Thalamus

Spinal cord

Relay nerve

Afferent nerve
Efferent nerve

Muscle

Skin

Stimulus

pain signal to reach the brain via the spinal cord, with the brain localising the signal after processing.

Sensitivity to pain varies for the different body regions. It is highest in the head and lowest in the foot region. It is also dependent on age and constitution.

Women are able to bear foreseeable pain better than men. People engaged in hard physical work or who keep themselves in good physical condition generally have a higher pain threshold than those who are only slightly or not at all physically active.

Reflex Arc

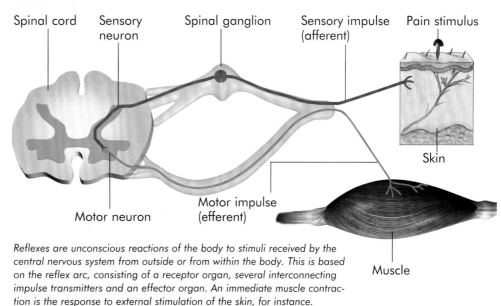

Spinal cord   Sensory neuron   Spinal ganglion   Sensory impulse (afferent)   Pain stimulus

Skin

Motor neuron   Motor impulse (efferent)

Muscle

Reflexes are unconscious reactions of the body to stimuli received by the central nervous system from outside or from within the body. This is based on the reflex arc, consisting of a receptor organ, several interconnecting impulse transmitters and an effector organ. An immediate muscle contraction is the response to external stimulation of the skin, for instance.

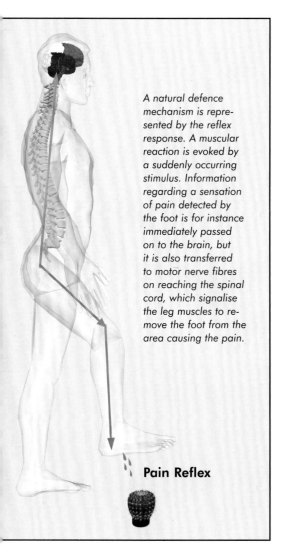

A natural defence mechanism is represented by the reflex response. A muscular reaction is evoked by a suddenly occurring stimulus. Information regarding a sensation of pain detected by the foot is for instance immediately passed on to the brain, but it is also transferred to motor nerve fibres on reaching the spinal cord, which signalise the leg muscles to remove the foot from the area causing the pain.

Pain Reflex

Reflexes

A reflex is an involuntary reaction by a muscle of the body to an externally applied stimulus. Reflexes involve a direct transmission of the excitation in the spinal cord to the motor nerve. In contrast to these are the conscious reactions, characterised by the information from the spinal cord being directed to the brain first, in order to receive further instructions.

A reflex is based on the reflex arc, a functional unit composed of several parts. The receiving organ (receptor) registers the information arriving from outside and transmits it via an afferent neuron (impulse transmitter), supplying the spinal cord with impulses. The signal is transferred from the sensory to the motor nerve cell via a point of connection, a junction known as a synapse. These impulses leave the spinal cord via an efferent neuron leading to the target organ.

This is exemplified by the knee-jerk reflex (patellar tendon reflex). The quadriceps femoral muscle is suddenly extended when the knee is tapped lightly with a reflex hammer. This extension is transmitted to the spinal cord via the neuromuscular spindles. Here, the motor anterior horn cells cause the contraction of the muscle.

Intrinsic reflexes of muscles generally occur within a single spinal cord segment. A sensory and a motor nerve cell are connected here (monosynaptic reflex). Extrinsic reflexes are characterised by the skin triggering muscle contraction. Stroking the abdominal skin will for instance cause the abdominal muscles to tense (abdominal reflex). This generally involves several nerve cells (several connection points/polysynaptic reflex).

Sensory Organs

Organ of Touch	64
Organ of Hearing and Balance	65
Organ of Vision	66–67
Organ of Taste	68
Organ of Smell	69

The sensory organs of the human body include the eye, the organ of balance and hearing, the organ of taste and the olfactory organ as well as the skin as the tactile organ.

The eyes *(oculi)* are located deep in the eye sockets *(orbita)*, which are formed by the bones of the skull. The one hundred million cells constituting our retina collect light and impressions from our general environment. This information is processed into what we see.

The human ear *(auris)* is able to hear a great number of different sounds. Hearing however only becomes possible in cooperation with the brain. Sound waves are converted to electrical nerve impulses and subsequently decoded by the brain. In association with the ear region, these nerve impulses also send signals regulating head movements and equilibrium.

Our sense of taste takes place via the tongue *(lingua)*. Taste buds that transmit signals to the gustatory centre in the brain are located there.

The skin, as a very sensitive sensory organ, possesses numerous tactile bodies (receptors and nerve ends) that react to touch, pain and temperature.

The sense of smell occurs via the nasal mucosa of the nose *(nasus)*. A small area of this contains a sensory cell layer, the olfactory epithelium. This detects smells and passes the information on to the brain.

All the information obtained by the brain from the principal sensory organs is generally referred to as sensory signals.

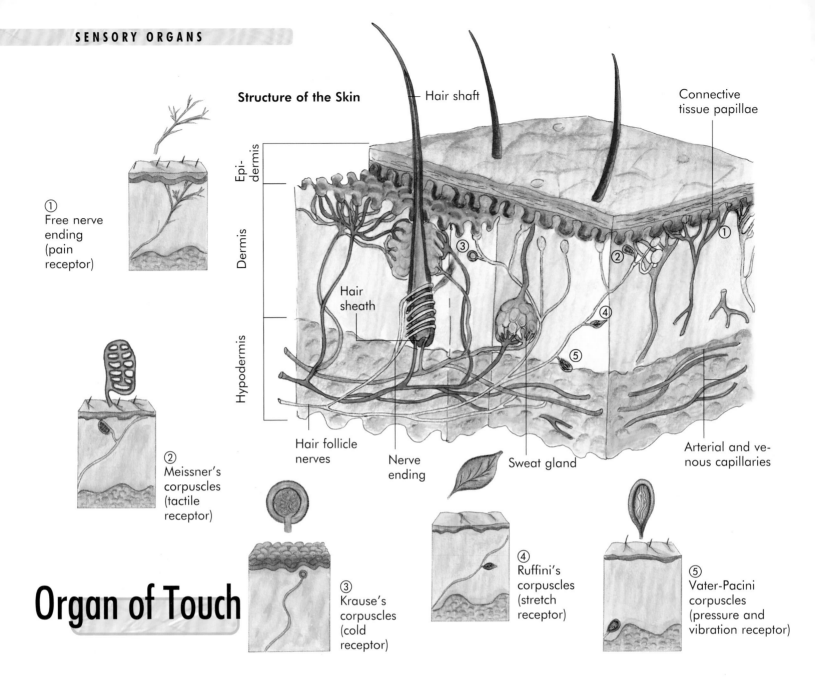

Structure of the Skin

Hair shaft

Connective tissue papillae

Epi-dermis

Dermis

Hypodermis

① Free nerve ending (pain receptor)

② Meissner's corpuscles (tactile receptor)

Hair sheath

③

②

④

⑤

①

Hair follicle nerves

Nerve ending

Sweat gland

Arterial and ve-nous capillaries

③ Krause's corpuscles (cold receptor)

④ Ruffini's corpuscles (stretch receptor)

⑤ Vater-Pacini corpuscles (pressure and vibration receptor)

Organ of Touch

The skin (cutis) covers the entire body and forms a barrier between body and environment. The surface of the skin has an area of 1.6–2.0 m² and a thickness of 1–4 mm. This vital organ forms the dermal system together with the nails and hair, and the mammary, scent, sweat and sebaceous glands. At body orifices, such as the mouth, the outer skin merges into mucous membrane.

The skin is divided into three sections:
• Epidermis (outer skin)
• Dermis
• Hypodermis (subcutis)

The primary functions of the skin include:
• Protection of the body from harmful influences
• Participation in thermal regulation (via the sweat glands)
• Communication of sensations.

A specialised tissue structure has developed in order to ensure the fulfilment of these numerous functions. In addition to epithelial cells and connective tissue cells, a fine network of branching nerves and blood vessels is found in the skin. The skin is the human body's largest sensory organ. It possesses numer-

ous specific receptors and nerve endings. These allow it to perceive stimuli elicited by touch, pressure, pain and temperature. Sensations of pressure are perceived via Merkel's tactile cells located at the junction of dermis and epidermis. Tactile sensations are registered by oval tactile corpuscles (Meissner's touch corpuscles) located in small pro-trusions (papillae) of the dermis, and by nerve plexuses around the hair root. Coldness is sensed by cold receptors (below 36 °C) while warmth is sensed by heat receptors (above 36 °C). Pain sensations are registered at the free nerve endings.

Organ of Hearing and Balance *(organum vestibulochochleare)*

Hearing has about the same significance for orientation in the environment as seeing. The ear assumes a special role in our communication based on spoken language. The ear is particularly sensitive to sound frequencies used for speech. Specific oscillations of the air are perceived by the organ of hearing.

The oscillations emitted from a body (sound waves) are absorbed by the air acting as a sound carrier, thereby allowing them to reach the ear. If these oscillations occur from 16 to no more than 20,000 times per second, then they are audible to human beings. Some animals have considerably better hearing capacities and are able to also register above 20,000 oscillations per second.

Low tones are created by slow oscillations, approximately 50 oscillations per second.

The highest audible tones have a maximum frequency of 20,000 oscillations per second. Oscillations exceeding this frequency are referred to as ultrasound.

They are not audible to the human ear.

The number of oscillations, and thereby also the pitch, is referred to as the frequency of the sound.

This is specified by means of the unit of measurement called hertz (Hz). One hertz corresponds to one oscillation per second. The maximum deviation of the sound wave from a quiescent state is referred to as the amplitude of the oscillation. Increasing amplitude implies a

loud sound, while decreasing amplitude implies a quiet sound. Loudness is measured in decibels (dB).

The oscillations of the air are converted to electrical nerve impulses in the ear, which in turn can be interpreted as sound by the brain. The ear also accommodates organs that communicate sensations regarding movement and position. It can be divided into three sections corresponding to its external structure. The sensory cells are located in the third section, the inner ear.

The inner ear includes:
- the cochlea with sensory cells for sound registration
- the semicircular duct with sensory cells for the perception of motion
- the two vestibular sacs with sensory cells for the perception of position

The organ of hearing is composed of the outer ear, middle ear and cochlea, while the organ of balance consists of the two vestibular sacs.

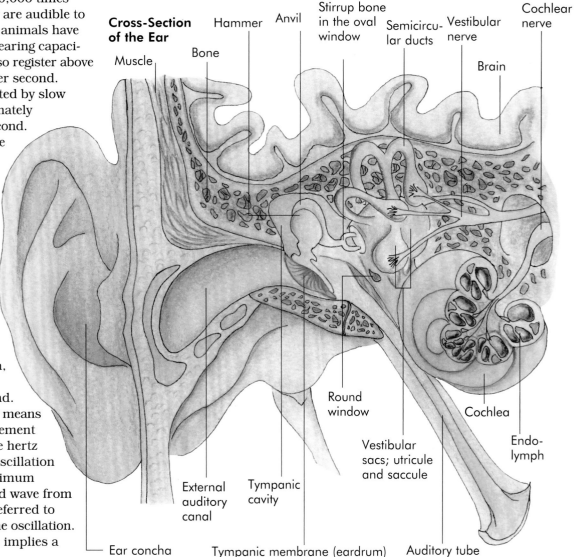

Cross-Section of the Ear

Muscle — Bone — Hammer — Anvil — Stirrup bone in the oval window — Semicircular ducts — Vestibular nerve — Cochlear nerve — Brain

Round window — Cochlea — Endolymph

External auditory canal — Tympanic cavity — Vestibular sacs; utricule and saccule

Ear concha — Tympanic membrane (eardrum) — Auditory tube

65

Organ of Vision *(organum visus)*

Light plays a crucial role in providing news and information relating to our surroundings. Seeing is one of the most important and complicated sensory perceptions used by human beings for orientation.

Light is the stimulus enabling the eyes *(oculi)* to distinguish between

Accommodation

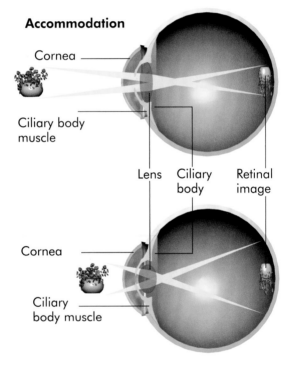

shapes and colours, lightness and darkness.

The actual process of seeing, however, takes place in the brain, where the stimuli initiated by light are processed. The highly developed form of this sensory perception is attributable to a great extent to the supportive function of memory.

The way a camera works is a popular analogy used for describing the visual process: the lens of the eye corresponds to the lens of the camera, the pupil to the camera aperture and the retina to the film. In the camera, a small-scale, upside-down image is obtained on the film through the

lens. An equivalent image is obtained on the retina of the eye.

The sensory cells of the visual organ *(organum visus)* are equipped with accessory features to form a complicated visual apparatus: optical stimuli are converted into nerve activity (neural excitation) in the eyeball *(bulbus oculi)*. These impulses are transported to the brain by means of an ingenious system of nerve fibres. The eye muscles *(musculi bulbi* or *ocular muscles)* allow slight movement of the eyeball *(bulbus oculi)*. The ability to see one image while using both eyes (binocular vision) is thereby achieved and the range of vision (visual field) can be enlarged. The lids, lashes, tear ducts and eyebrows are the protective organs of the eyeball.

Visual Process – The parts of the eye involved in the refraction of light include the cornea *(keratoderma* of the eye), the aqueous humour (intraocular fluid), the lens and the vitreous humour (or body). When light rays reach the eye through the

Visual Pathway

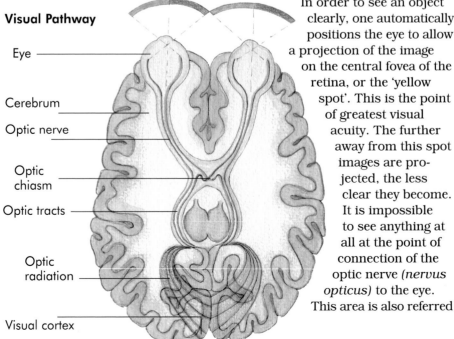

eye's refractive section, they are united to produce a single image by conversion of the bundled rays of light to neural impulses. These are subsequently transported to the visual centre of the brain, with the result that the image is consciously perceived.

In order to see an object clearly, one automatically positions the eye to allow a projection of the image on the central fovea of the retina, or the 'yellow spot'. This is the point of greatest visual acuity. The further away from this spot images are projected, the less clear they become. It is impossible to see anything at all at the point of connection of the optic nerve *(nervus opticus)* to the eye. This area is also referred

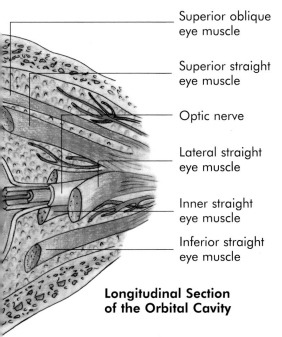

Superior oblique eye muscle

Superior straight eye muscle

Optic nerve

Lateral straight eye muscle

Inner straight eye muscle

Inferior straight eye muscle

Longitudinal Section of the Orbital Cavity

Farsightedness (hyperopia)

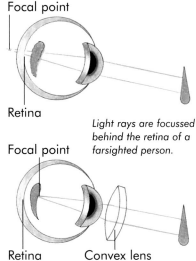

Focal point

Retina

Light rays are focussed behind the retina of a farsighted person.

Focal point

Retina Convex lens

Astigmatism

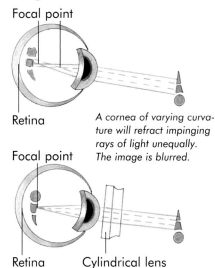

Focal point

Retina

A cornea of varying curvature will refract impinging rays of light unequally. The image is blurred.

Focal point

Retina Cylindrical lens

to as the 'blind spot'. An eye capable of normal vision will automatically produce a clear image on the retina when looking into the distance. Light has to be refracted much more in order to obtain a sharp image of an object located nearer to the eye. This is achieved by changing the curvature of the lens. The ability to adapt to the distance at which an object being observed is located is known as the accommodative capacity of the lens. This, in conjunction with the ability of the pupil to alter the depth of field of the lens, also contributes to the focussing process.

It must however also be taken into consideration that all this normally takes place simultaneously in each eye (binocular). In order to avoid double vision (diplopia), the brain is capable of merging the images. This process is referred to as fusion.

Visual Defects

An eye of normal structure that is capable of normal vision will focus the rays of light on the retina to provide a sharp image. The eyeball

may, however, be too short or too long. This will result in the rays being focussed either in front of or behind the retina, with the consequence that an unclear image is obtained.

An eyeball that is too short in structure will focus the rays behind the retina. This is called farsightedness or longsightedness *(hyperopia)*. An eyeball that is too long in structure will focus the rays in front of the centre of the retina. This is called shortsightedness or nearsightedness *(myopia)*. A further visual defect is represented by a cornea deviating

from the normal spherical shape. This will result in the refractive power of the eye varying for the different meridians.

This is referred to as astigmia or astigmatism. Instead of being perceived sharply, objects are distorted or blurred.

Farsightedness may be corrected during youth. The ability of the eye to focus on nearby objects (accommodative capacity) is increasingly reduced with age, due to the lens becoming less elastic. Difficulties are experienced when reading. This is known as presbyopia (old sight).

Shortsightedness (myopia)

Focal point

Retina

An image is formed in front of the retina of a shortsighted person. A blurred image results.

Focal point

Retina Concave lens

Presbyopia (old sight)

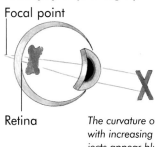

Focal point

Retina

The curvature of the lens changes with increasing age. Nearby objects appear blurred.

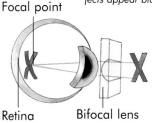

Focal point

Retina Bifocal lens

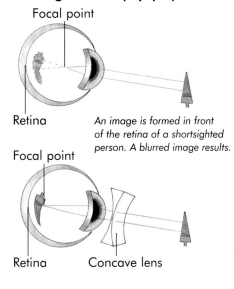

Organ of Taste *(organum gustus)*

The gustatory organ does not have a closed structure. Its 2,000 taste buds are located in the tissue of the tongue and palate, the epiglottis and the upper oesophagus. Most of them are situated in the vallate papillae in the mucous membrane of the tongue.

Taste buds are 40 μm wide and 80 μm high. There are about 250 taste buds per vallate papilla in children and young individuals, while people of an advanced age only have about 80. Each taste bud has 30–80 receptor cells. These are composed of supporting, basal and sensory cells, which are constantly being renewed.

Taste receptors do not possess their own nerve fibres, but are connected to nerve fibres in the tongue by means of synapses. The nerve fibres form bundles and follow the seventh and ninth cranial nerves to nerve cells located in the brainstem. Conduction and processing in the thalamus is followed by final processing in the cerebral cortex.

The tip of the taste bud features a recess, opening to the tongue surface by means of a taste pore.

This aperture allows fluids from the substance being tasted to reach the sensory cells.

Taste cells are chemoreceptors, the detailed mode of action of which is as yet unclear. Only four different qualities of taste can be distinguished: sweet, sour, bitter and salty. The range of sensations actually perceived is increased by their combination. The different taste types are registered by appropriate receptors distributed in specific areas of the tongue. The tip of tongue is able to taste sweet substances, the edges of the tongue salty and sour substances, while the base of the tongue is able to detect bitter substances.

Our sense of taste is not highly developed. Delicate differences may however be distinguished thanks to the cooperation of the sense of taste with the sense of smell. A nose blocked due to a cold will prevent us from smelling anything and impair our sense of taste drastically.

Taste Zones of the Tongue

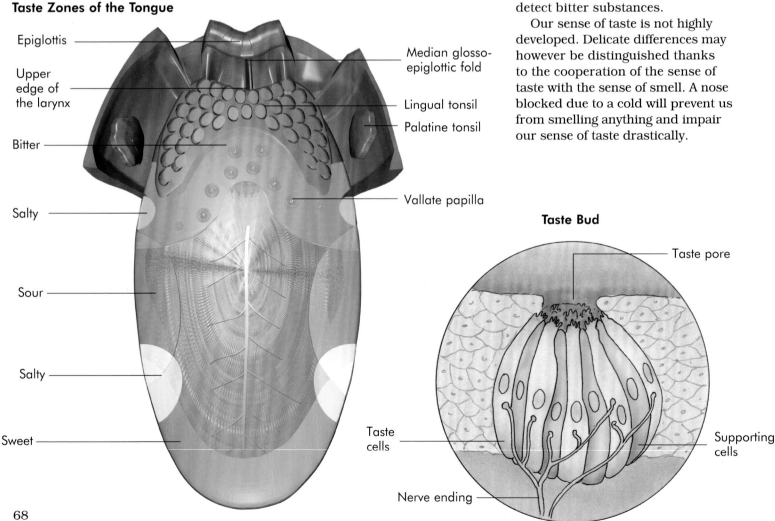

Epiglottis

Upper edge of the larynx

Bitter

Salty

Sour

Salty

Sweet

Median glosso-epiglottic fold

Lingual tonsil

Palatine tonsil

Vallate papilla

Taste Bud

Taste pore

Taste cells

Nerve ending

Supporting cells

Organ of Smell *(organum olfactus)*

The olfactory organ is located at the beginning of the respiratory passage, occupying an area the size of a coin almost 2 cm in diameter near the superior nasal concha and the neighbouring nasal septum.

The olfactory region has a yellow colour due to pigment deposits, thereby standing out from the surrounding red mucosa. It is unclear whether the pigments are involved in the smelling process. It is however known that animals lacking pigments (albinos) have no sense of smell. The epithelium of the olfactory region (over 10 million receptor cells) is about 50 μm higher than the respiratory epithelium.

Each olfactory cell is equipped with up to 12 very fine hairs (cilia) and covered with mucus. Nerve processes lead as fibre bundles from the olfactory cells to the anterior section of the olfactory brain (rhinencephalon) located at the base of the frontal brain. The olfactory cells are separated from the olfactory brain by means of a wafer-thin bone, the sieve plate, allowing the passage of the nerve fibres through its perforations. Awareness of a smell is achieved after appropriate processing of information.

Olfactory cells are chemoreceptors, i.e. excitation of the sensory cells is a consequence of chemical processes at the surface of the cilia. The molecular reaction involved for the differentiation of hundreds of different sensations of smell has however not yet been elucidated.

Gaseous substances are detected more easily. Solubility in water also enhances olfactory registration, since the scent molecules are released into the air on evaporation. The perfume industry makes use of this principle.

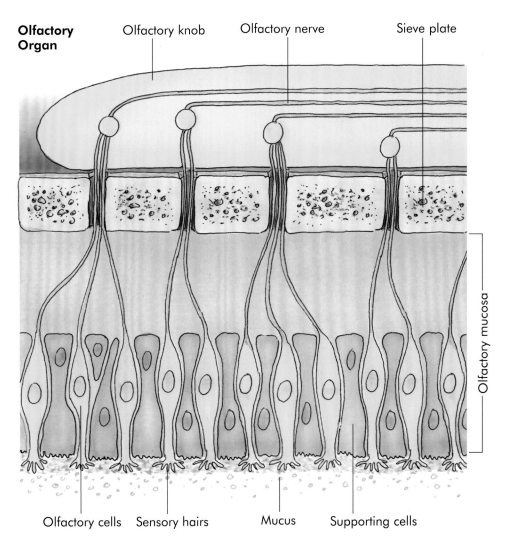

Olfactory Organ — Olfactory knob, Olfactory nerve, Sieve plate, Olfactory mucosa, Olfactory cells, Sensory hairs, Mucus, Supporting cells

The perception of fine differences in smell can be trained, with an experienced perfumer able to distinguish over 5,000 different smells. A persistent smell fails to be detected after some time, because the olfactory sensation fatigues.

It is presumed that all receptors are occupied by the particular odour substance and need a period of recovery. Olfactory cells die after about 4 weeks and are replaced by new ones. The dead cells are discharged with the mucus.

No definitive designations exist for the classification of smells.

They are generally specified according to their sources, e.g. scent of violets, burning smell. Many animals have an extremely well-developed sense of smell. A dog possesses about ten times more olfactory cells than a human being; a dog's nose is his most important sensory organ.

The olfactory brain is closely associated with the limbic system. This association explains why some smells are regarded as pleasant, while others elicit disgust, and why we connect certain smells with specific events.

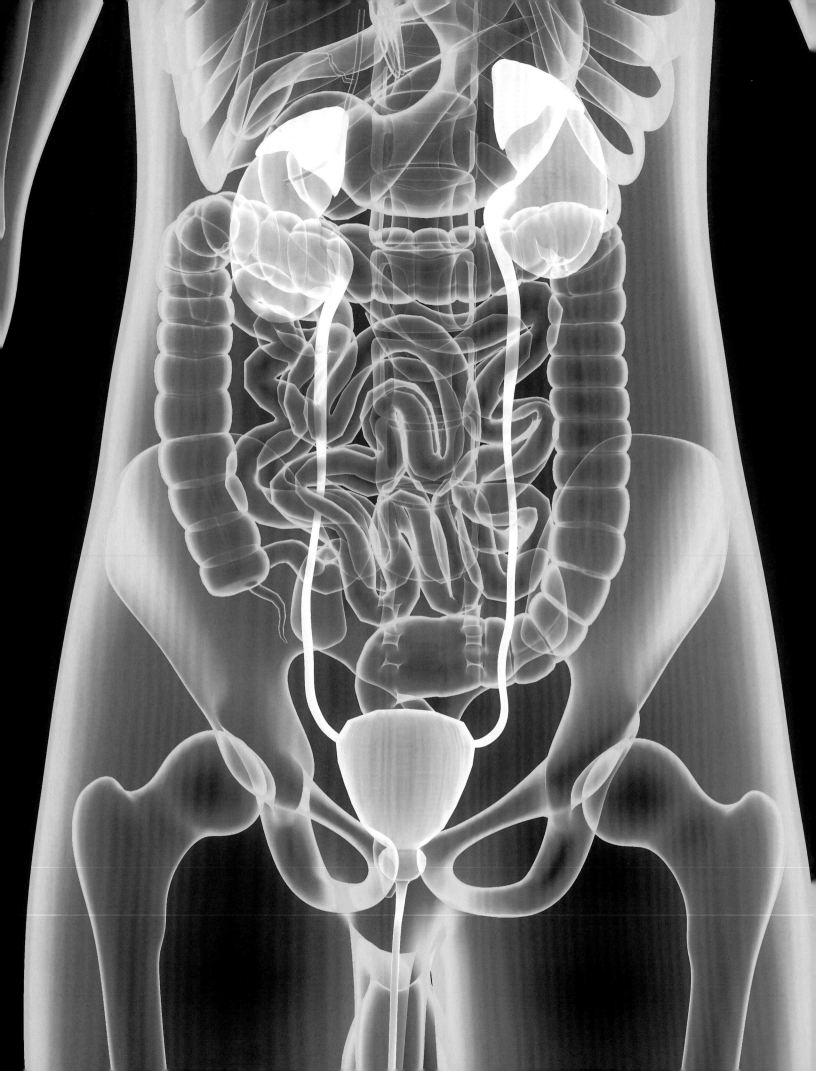

CHAPTER 8

Kidneys/ Urinary System

Kidneys	**72–73**
Nephrons	**73–74**
Ureters	**74**
Urinary Bladder	**74**
Male Urethra	**75**
Female Urethra	**75**

Besides the lungs, the skin and the intestines, the kidneys are the most important excretory organs of the body.

All products from cellular metabolism that are not usable by the body are transported to the kidneys by the blood and filtered out of the blood plasma there. The products are then eliminated via the urine (micturition).

Urine is formed in the kidneys, or more specifically in over one million small filters, the nephrons. After several filtration processes taking place at various stages, the urine is excreted via the ureter, the bladder and finally the urethra.

Kidneys (ren)

Each of the two kidneys is located in the lumbar region next to the spinal column, behind the connective tissue of the abdominal cavity (retroperitoneal space) and protected by the lower ribs. Each kidney is 10–12 cm long, 2–4 cm thick, 5–6 cm wide and weighs 120–300 g.

The inner curvature of the bean-shaped kidney forms an indentation *(sinus renalis)*. Blood and lymph vessels, nerves and the renal pelvis lead into the first section of the ureter here.

Each kidney is surrounded by a firm envelope, the renal capsule *(capsula fibrosa)*. This is embedded in a fatty capsule *(capsula adiposa)*. The adipose capsule forms a cushion for the kidney, the renal bed, protecting it from heat loss and from blows.

The function of the kidneys is intimately linked to that of the vascular system. The amount of blood flowing through a kidney in one minute is almost more than double its own weight. In a quiescent state, only some of the renal corpuscles are perfused with blood. The afferent and efferent vessels influence renal perfusion by means of mechanisms for slowing down the blood-flow. The tissue hormones are also involved in this process.

Two distinct layers can be observed in a longitudinal section of renal tissue. The renal cortex *(cortex renalis)*, located next to the renal capsule, is a granular reddish brown zone, with a thickness of about 6–10 mm. The renal corpuscles responsible for blood filtration are situated within the cortex.

A uriniferous (or renal) tubule *(tubuli renales)* emerges from each renal (or malphigian) corpuscle. The filtered fluid is prepared for elimi-

nation by means of a complicated metabolic process here. Renal corpuscle and renal tubule constitute the smallest functional unit of the kidney, the nephron.

The renal medulla does not form a coherent layer, but consists of 7–20 finely striped, renal pyramids surrounded by cortical substance.

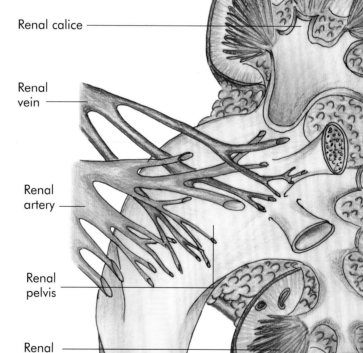

The uriniferous tubules are located in the renal medulla. The renal medulla of the broader end of the pyramids, runs into the

cortex, resulting in a stripy appearance, known as the medullary rays. The pointed ends of the pyramids, the renal papillae, jut into the

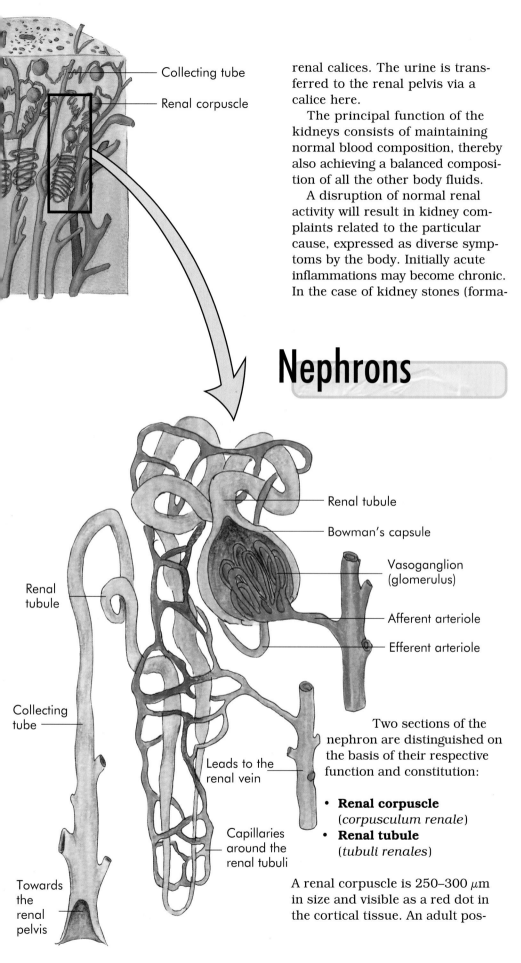

Collecting tube

Renal corpuscle

Renal tubule

Bowman's capsule

Vasoganglion
(glomerulus)

Afferent arteriole

Efferent arteriole

Renal
tubule

Collecting
tube

Leads to the
renal vein

Capillaries
around the
renal tubuli

Towards
the
renal
pelvis

Nephrons

renal calices. The urine is transferred to the renal pelvis via a calice here.

The principal function of the kidneys consists of maintaining normal blood composition, thereby also achieving a balanced composition of all the other body fluids.

A disruption of normal renal activity will result in kidney complaints related to the particular cause, expressed as diverse symptoms by the body. Initially acute inflammations may become chronic. In the case of kidney stones (forma- tion chiefly due to inappropriate diet or hyperactive parathyroid glands), symptoms observed depend on the size and the position of the renal calculus (kidney stone), generally including severe abdominal pain, accompanied by nausea and dark or cloudy urine that may contain blood. Kidney failure may occur in extreme cases. Treatment is possible by means of a dialysis machine, which is able to take over the work of the kidneys, or by transplantation of a kidney from another person.

Two sections of the nephron are distinguished on the basis of their respective function and constitution:

- **Renal corpuscle**
  (*corpusculum renale*)
- **Renal tubule**
  (*tubuli renales*)

A renal corpuscle is 250–300 μm in size and visible as a red dot in the cortical tissue. An adult possesses about 2.5 million renal corpuscles.

A vasoganglion *(glomerulus)* composed of very fine capillaries is enclosed by a waterproof capsule *(capsula glomeruli)*, known as a Bowman's capsule (alt. glomerular or malphigian capsule). The blood in the glomerule is filtered through the pores of the vessels and the cellular gaps in the Bowman's capsule. Very small substances such as minerals, urea, creatinine (metabolic product from muscle tissue) and glucose pass through the filter during glomerular filtration. Blood cells and protein molecules are too large for the filter perforations and remain in the blood. An increase in size of the perforations (due for instance to an inflammation) will allow these to enter the filtrate and be detected in the urine.

The filtered fluid, the primary urine, is collected by the Bowman's capsule and passed on to the adjoining renal (or uriniferous) tubules. About 125 ml of primary urine is formed every minute on average, which is 170–180 litres every 24 hours. The renal tubules are responsible for reabsorption of substances dissolved in the primary

73

urine, which are essential for the body. The renal tubules start off convoluted, continuing downwards, then upwards and downwards again. On the basis of varying morphological composition, different functions are carried out by the various sections (proximal tubule, distal tubule and collecting tubule) during the process of reabsorption.

The **proximal tubule** is responsible for reabsorption of the majority of salts and water and returning these to the blood. Further water reabsorption takes place in the **distal tubule**. Electrolytes are reabsorbed in the **collecting tube**. Concentration of urine is completed and the end-product (urine) is formed. About 1.5 litres of urine are produced in

this manner every 24 hours, for elimination by the body. The volume of urine depends on external influencing factors such as intake of liquids by means of nutrition, and physical activity.

Ureters

The two ureters are approximately 25 cm-long tubes with a diameter of 5 mm, which conduct urine from the renal pelvis into the bladder. Commencing from the renal pelvis of the kidneys, they lead through the abdominal wall, cross the blood vessels (vasa sanguinea) of the pelvis, and finally enter through the bladder wall (vesica urinaria)

in order to discharge their contents into the bladder.

Each ureter is composed of three layers. The inside is covered with a mucous membrane (tunica mucosa). This is followed by a muscular layer (tunica muscularis). The mucosa is responsible for the distensible nature of the bladder. The wave-like movement of the musculature, about

1–4 times per minute, (peristalsis) allows the urine to be transported.

The final layer is composed of a connective tissue coat (tunica adventitia), accommodating various blood vessels and nerves. The outer cover connects each ureter to its immediate surroundings, at the same time permitting a certain degree of mobility.

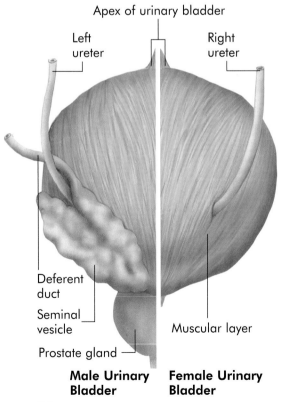

Apex of urinary bladder

Left ureter

Right ureter

Deferent duct

Seminal vesicle

Prostate gland

Muscular layer

Male Urinary Bladder　　**Female Urinary Bladder**

Urinary Bladder (vesica urinaria)

The urine eliminated by the kidneys is collected in the urinary bladder. The average kidney volume is about 500 ml, while maximum capacity varies according to individual training. The urge to urinate is felt from about 200 ml. A full bladder has a spherical shape, an empty one resembles a saggy bag.

The bladder may be divided into four sections:
• The apex of the bladder or vertex (connection to the navel via an umbilical tendon)

• the body of the bladder constituting the major part of the bladder wall
• the fundus of the bladder (base)
• the neck of the bladder from which the urethra emerges.

The apex and posterior and lateral parts of the body of the urinary bladder are covered with peritoneum. Emptying of the urinary bladder is mainly controlled by the voluntary sphincter muscle of the urethra. Urinary incontinence is the consequence of a paralysis of this muscle.

Male Urethra *(urethra masculina)*

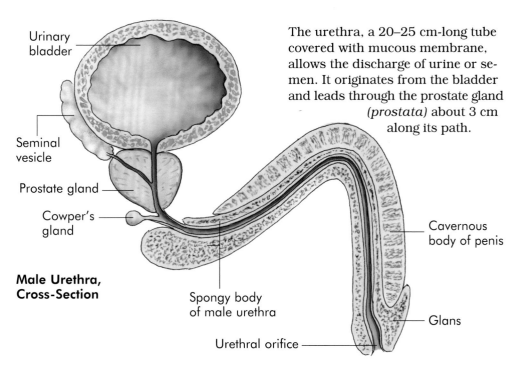

Urinary bladder

Seminal vesicle

Prostate gland

Cowper's gland

Male Urethra, Cross-Section

Spongy body of male urethra

Urethral orifice

Cavernous body of penis

Glans

The urethra, a 20–25 cm-long tube covered with mucous membrane, allows the discharge of urine or semen. It originates from the bladder and leads through the prostate gland *(prostata)* about 3 cm along its path.

The excretory ducts of the the vas deferens *(ductus deferens)* and the genital glands join the urethra here, which is why it is really a urinary-seminal duct from this point onwards.

This is followed by a short section running through the pelvic floor. Surrounded by the cavernous bodies of the penis *(corpus cavernosum penis)* and the spongy bodies of the male urethra *(corpus spongiosum penis)*, the urethra then passes through the penis, finally terminating at the tip of the penis.

The section just before the entry of the urethra into the penis is surrounded by muscle fibres forming the urethral sphincter muscle.

Female Urethra *(Urethra feminina)*

The female urethra originates from the neck of the bladder and is located in front of the uterus and vagina. It crosses the pelvic floor, and, running alongside the anterior vaginal wall, then leads into the vestibule of the vagina *(vestibulum vaginae)* on a small protrusion below the clitoris.

In contrast to the male urethra *(urethra masculina)*, the female urethra is only about 3–4 cm long, follows a straight path and transports only urine.

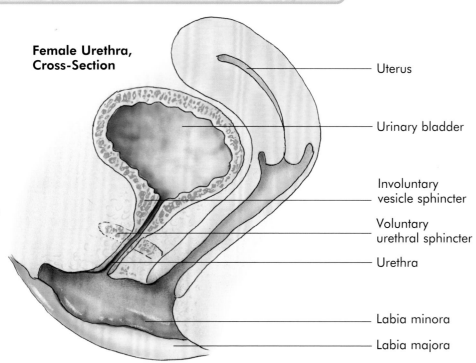

Female Urethra, Cross-Section

Uterus

Urinary bladder

Involuntary vesicle sphincter

Voluntary urethral sphincter

Urethra

Labia minora

Labia majora

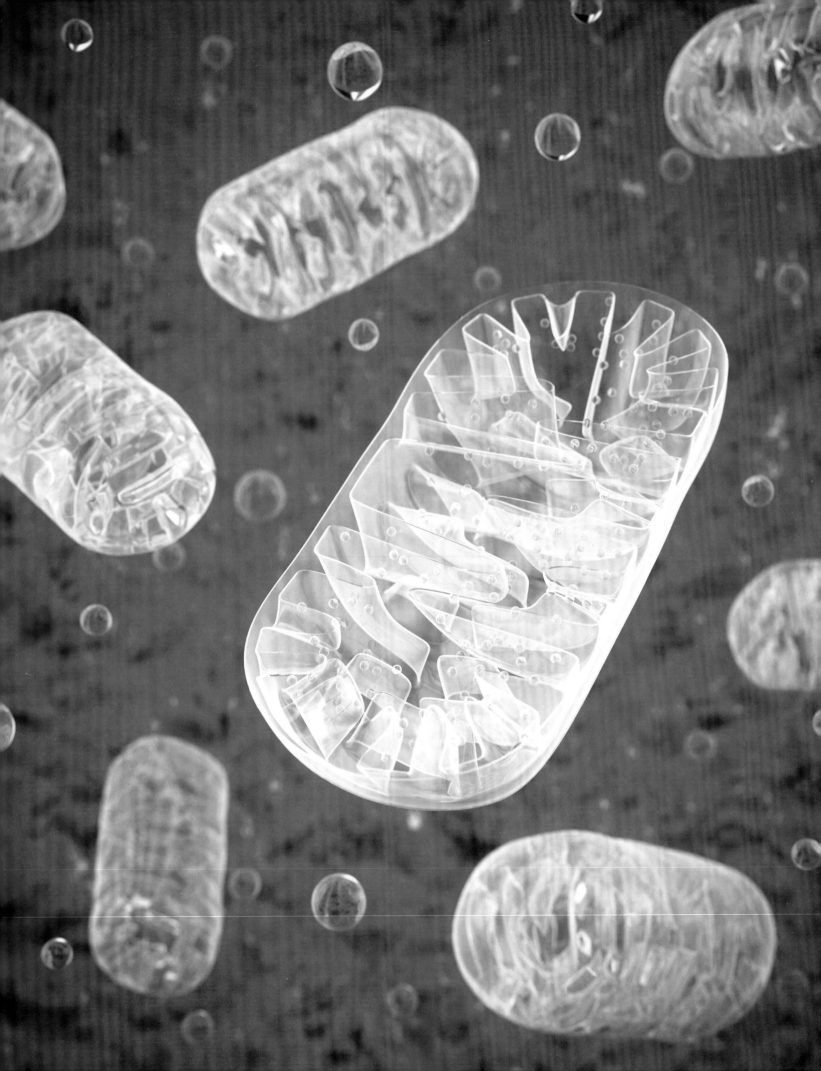

Cells

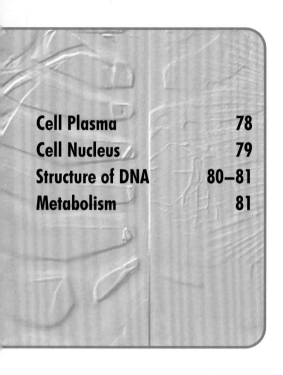

Cell Plasma	78
Cell Nucleus	79
Structure of DNA	80–81
Metabolism	81

The cell is the body's smallest structural and functional unit. The limited independent life of a cell, with its own material and energy exchange, is under the influence of the nerve and blood systems.

The cells of the human body cooperate with each other in the fulfilment of their various functions. They have various shapes and forms, depending on their specific activities. The cell consists of protoplasm and is divided into cytoplasm (cell plasma) and a nucleus (nucleoplasm). Cells without a nucleus are only capable of surviving for a short period of time, such as red blood cells. Nuclei expelled from cells are also unable to survive. A cell membrane *(cytolemma)* separates the cell body from its immediate environment.

The nucleus is chiefly composed of chromosomes. These are the carriers of genetic material and are made up mainly of deoxyribonucleic acid (DNA). The nucleus is responsible for the transfer of genetic properties to the daughter cells and hence to the following generations. It simultaneously functions as the metabolic centre of the cell.

The interaction of cell body and nucleus is expressed as the nucleocytoplasmic ratio. The cell will die if this relationship is disturbed. Cells also vary in size, as dictated by their different functions. The circumference of a cell ranges from 5–200 μm. Cells reproduce by means of cell division *(mitosis)*. The cell divides itself by a constriction, pinching the cell body apart.

Egg and sperm cells divide by means of a special process called meiosis. This ensures that egg and sperm cells with half a chromosome complement (haploid) are produced.

Cell Plasma (cytoplasma)

The plasma of the cell is composed of a fluid containing up to 60% water, the cytoplasm, which is surrounded by a thin coat, the cell membrane (*membrana cellularis*). The cell membrane allows the exchange of substances from outside the cell (*cellula*) to inside the cell and vice versa.

In addition to the ground substance (hyaloplasm), the cytoplasm also contains various microscopic organs, known as the cell organelles, which differ in structure and function.

Mitochondria (*mitochondrion*) are responsible for supplying energy to the cell, and are therefore also referred to as cellular 'power stations'. The combustion of nutrients such as sugar and fat, which enter the cell, takes place in the mitochondria, with the help of oxygen. The energy released by this process is stored in the form of the substance ATP (adenosine triphosphate), and provided for utilisation by the cell in the execution of its tasks, such as metabolic activity or muscular movement.

The **endoplasmic reticulum** (*reticulum endoplasmaticum*) consists of a membrane running through the cytoplasm, which is folded up to form small canals, thereby allowing the transportation of substances.

Small structures, the **ribosomes**, are often attached to the canals, but may also be observed in the cytoplasm individually. Proteins are produced with the aid of the substance contained in the ribosomes, RNA (ribonucleic acid). The protein molecules are packaged in small vesicles for transportation, which are made of the membrane of the endoplasmic reticulum.

A further system of small ducts is represented by the Golgi body (*complexus golgiensis*). This permits the uptake and removal of substances and is therefore divided into an input and an output side.

The proteins produced in the ribosomes are taken up by the **Golgi body** via the input side, and after processing leave the cell via the output side of the Golgi body (alt. apparatus or complex). The Golgi body furthermore ensures that harmful substances that may represent a threat to the cell are enveloped.

Vesicular **lysosomes** are further cytoplasmic components, produced in the endoplasmic reticulum and the Golgi body. Lysosomes are responsible for breaking down foreign bodies that have been taken up, or cellular organelles that have ceased to be operational, with the aid of enzymes.

The **centrioles**, of which there are generally two in number, play an important role in cell division (*divisio cellularis*).

Depending on the type of cell, cytoplasm may contain metaplasm or paraplasm. **Metaplasm** includes structural components called fibrils. There are three types of fibrils, located in different cells depending on their function. The myofibrils are located in muscle cells, neurofibrils in nerve cells and tonofibrils in tissue.

Paraplasm (or hyaloplasm) contains metabolic products such as fats, carbohydrates and secretions, representing either material reserves or breakdown products. The term protoplasm is used for a living active cell.

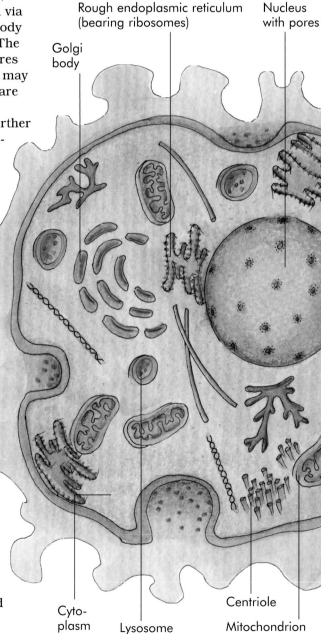

Golgi body

Rough endoplasmic reticulum (bearing ribosomes)

Nucleus with pores

Cytoplasm

Lysosome

Centriole

Mitochondrion

Cell Nucleus

As carrier of hereditary characteristics, the nucleus of the cell is the control centre of cellular metabolism. Each cell (cellula) normally contains a nucleus. Cells that lack a nucleus (anucleate), such as red blood cells (erythrocytes), are consequently capable of surviving for a limited period of time only, and are unable to divide.

The size and shape of the nucleus depends on the type of cell and its function and also the stage of development of the cell. It may for instance be round or longitudinal in shape. All nuclear structures are duplicated before and during cell division (mitosis) and distributed to the daughter cells.

The nucleus of a cell between two divisions is called an interphase nucleus. It is surrounded by a coat, the nuclear membrane, separating it from the cytoplasm, and also allowing substance exchange between nucleus and cytoplasm.

One to two round structures are found within the nucleus of the cell, the nucleoli (micronuclei). These chiefly contain ribonucleic acid (RNA), a constituent that primarily plays a role in protein synthesis. The nucleoli are embedded in the nuclear plasma, composed mainly of chromatin (chromoplasm or karyotin). During cell division, the chromosomes carrying the genetic information (genes) arise from the chromatin. Thousands of genes are contained in one chromosome.

Human beings possess a species-specific chromosome complement. This is composed of 22 chromosome pairs (autosomes) and two sex chromosomes (gonosomes), i.e. a total of 46 chromosomes (diploid chromosome number). Each pair of chromosomes is composed of one paternal and one maternal chromosome.

The sex chromosomes are called X and Y chromosomes. The female gender is characterised by two X chromosomes. If the fertilising sperm cell (spermium) contains a Y chromosome, then a boy will be produced. If the sperm cell introduces an X chromosome, then a girl will develop.

The sperm and egg (ovum) cells are subject to a special reduction division (meiosis). This ensures the production of two cells each containing only half a chromosome set (haploid chromosome number). Fertilisation (fecundation) will result in a cell containing one chromosome complement from the father and one from the mother.

Interphase

Early prophase 1

Middle prophase 1

Late prophase 1

Metaphase 1

Anaphase 1

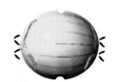
Telophase 1

Telophase 2

Anaphase 2

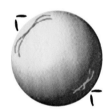
Metaphase 2

Prophase 2

Meiosis, also known as reduction division, is a special form of cell division. This involves the female and male germ cells halving their chromosome complements, in order to ensure that the fusion of sperm and egg cells results in a normal, i.e. diploid chromosome complement. This complicated process includes a first and second reduction division, finally resulting in mature sex cells (gametes).

79

Structure of DNA

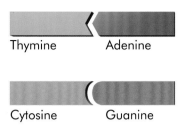

Each of the chromosomes contained in the nucleus of a human cell consists of two chromosome arms connected by a constriction (centromere). These contain chromatin, which becomes more condensed and forms spiral-shaped strands, the chromatids, just before cell division. The chromatids contain the molecule deoxyribonucleic acid, DNA, the carrier of genetic information (genes).

The structure of DNA resembles a spiral staircase, and is referred to as 'double helix' for this reason. It is composed of two thin strands connected to each other by cross-linkages. The individual structural elements of this spiral staircase are the nucleotides. Each nucleotide is composed of three parts: a sugar, a phosphate and a nitrogen-containing base – adenine, thymine, cytosine or guanine.

The two bases adenine and thymine, connected via two hydrogen molecules, and the two bases cytosine and guanine, connected via three hydrogen molecules, represent the steps of the spiral staircase. Phosphate forms the railing and sugar is the connecting piece linking each step with the railing.

DNA Replication – The cellular DNA is replicated just before the actual process of division of the cell by mitosis. The base pairs that connected the two DNA strands of the original double helix with each other as cross-linkages break off at their site of connection – the hydrogen bridge. This results in two single strands with half steps. The bases of the nucleotides becoming available in the process, however, reconnect to their base partners located on the two single strands (adenine with thymine and guanine

Thymine   Adenine

Cytosine   Guanine

 Phosphoric acid

■ Desoxyribose

with cytosine) to form a complete step, with the complementary nucleotides associating. Two new single strands are thereby formed, which connect with the existing single strands.

Mitosis – The process of cell division of body cells is called mitosis. Two identical new cells are produced from one cell as a result. The nucleus of a cell accommodates a diploid chromosome complement consisting of 22 identical chromosome pairs (homologous chromosomes) and two sex chromosomes (heterologous chromosomes). The set is replicated just before cell division, producing chromosomes consisting of two chromatids. Mitosis is divided into four phases:

- **Prophase**
- **Metaphase**
- **Anaphase**
- **Telophase**

During **prophase**, the nuclear membrane surrounding the now no longer visible nucleus of the cell body disappears. The already replicated chromosomes, now consisting of two chromatids connected by means of a constriction (*centromere*), take on a spiral shape and become visible. Each of the two centrioles of the original cell migrates to a cell

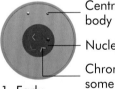

Central body

Nucleus

Chromosome

1. Early prophase

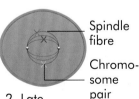

4. Early anaphase

7. Late telophase

Spindle fibre

Chromosome pair

2. Late prophase

5. Late anaphase

8. Interphase

3. Metaphase

6. Early telophase

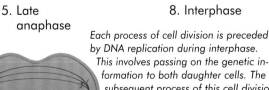

Each process of cell division is preceded by DNA replication during interphase. This involves passing on the genetic information to both daughter cells. The subsequent process of this cell division, called mitosis, is divided into prophase, metaphase, anaphase and telophase, after the completion of which two independent daughter cells of the same size are produced.

The DNA, bearing the genetic information, is composed of three main parts: The side parts are made up of sugar and phosphate molecules. The cross-linkages are composed of nitrogen-containing bases linked by hydrogen molecules.

pole, situated opposite to each other. They form thin fibres known as the spindle apparatus.

At the start of the second phase, the **metaphase**, the chromatids are shortened to the greatest extent and become visible by electron microscopy. They assume a central position in the cell body (equatorial plane).

In the course of the following **anaphase**, the chromatids separate from the centromere and migrate to the poles, resulting in an identical chromosome complement located at each pole.

During the final phase, the **telophase**, the chromosomes located at the two cell poles become invisible again through de-spiralisation.

They form the respective nucleus surrounded by a nuclear membrane of each daughter (or secondary) cell. The cytoplasm of the original cell is divided in the middle by constriction, resulting in two new daughter cells with 23 pairs of chromosomes each.

The mitotic division of body cells therefore allows growth and the regeneration of dead cells. All cells are renewed by mitosis on a regular basis, except for nerve and sex cells.

Metabolism

Nutritional components produced by the process of digestion are absorbed by the cell via the blood in the course of metabolism. These are converted to cellular substances, while substances that are not needed are eliminated as waste products. Cell respiration is essential for these processes, requiring oxygen uptake and carbon dioxide removal. Metabolism is classified into two different types of metabolism, **assimilatory metabolism** and **dissimilatory metabolism**.

The inside of the cell is provided with nutritive elements by means of vesicular transport (cytopempsis). Unwanted substances are also removed by this route. The components are packaged with a material made of membrane components and imported into the cell as enveloped vesicles *(endocytosis)* and also removed to the exterior of the cell *(exocytosis)*. This process is referred to as phagocytosis.

Assimilatory metabolism therefore allows ingested nutrient elements to be processed into endogenous material and used for cell construction. Dissimilatory metabolism involves the breakdown of nutrient substances and unneeded materials into carbon dioxide, urea and water. The energy-rich substance ATP, released by this process, is stored in the body temporarily.

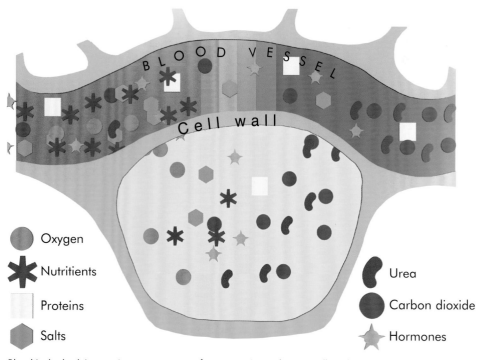

Blood is the body's most important means of transport. It supplies our cells with oxygen and nutrients. At the same time, it removes carbon dioxide and other waste products from the cell.

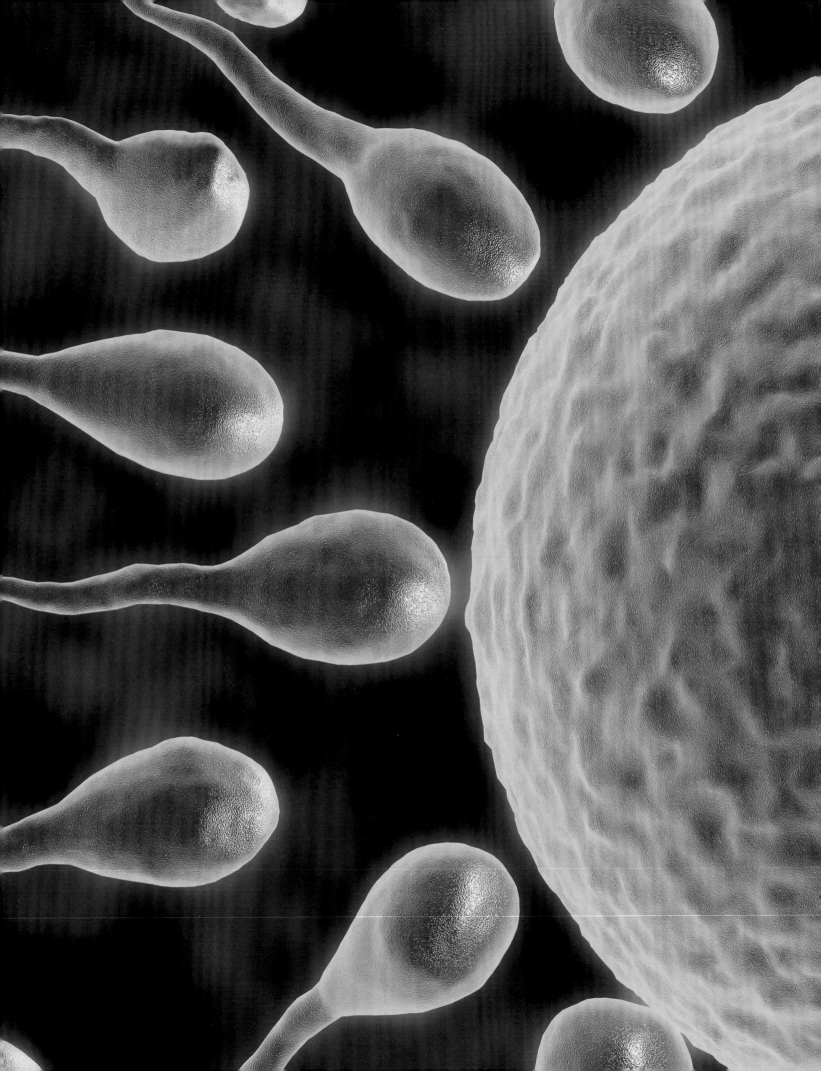

CHAPTER 10

Reproduction

Male
Genital Organs   84–85

Female
Genital Organs   86–88

Reproduction   88–89

Pregnancy   90–91

Birth   92–93

Human sexual reproduction is based on the fusion of the male sperm cell with the female egg cell, which is called conception *(fecundatio)*. After the subsequent journey through the oviduct, the ovum (now a zygote) implants itself in the uterine mucosa (endometrium) and develops into a viable baby after completion of an embryonic and a foetal phase.

The process of giving birth is divided into a first (dilation) and second (expulsion) stage of labour, resulting in the passage of the infant through the maternal pelvis on its way outside.

Male Genital Organs

The male genital organs are divided into the internal and external genitalia.

The external organs include
• the penis
• the scrotum

The internal organs are subdivided into
• the testicles (*testis*/*testes*)
• the epididymis (*pl.* epididymides)
• the deferent duct (*vas deferens*)
• the seminal vesicle (*vesicula seminalis*)
• the prostate gland (*prostata*).

Penis

The penis is the male copulative organ, since it allows the introduction of sperm into the female body during the sexual act between man and woman.

It is divided into root, shaft and glans. The root, covered with muscles and skin, is firmly attached to the pelvic floor. Three regions of erectile tissue are located in the mobile part of the penis: two penile cavernous bodies (*corpus cavernosum penis*) on the outer sides and a urethral spongy body (*corpus spongiosum penis*), which encloses the urethra that passes through the entire penis. The urethral spongy body ends as the glans at the front end of the penis.

Each spongy or cavernous body consists of connective tissue, muscle fibres and hollow spaces (caverns) located in between, with small arteries (*arteriae*) leading into these. Sexual arousal results in these caverns being filled with

Their function consists of, on the one hand, the formation of germ cells (gametes) and sex hormones for transportation via the sexual pathways, and on the other, the facilitation of sexual intercourse by means of the external sexual organs.

Secretions are furthermore produced in the genital glands, which are favourable for the unification of sperm and egg cells.

Position of the Prostate Gland

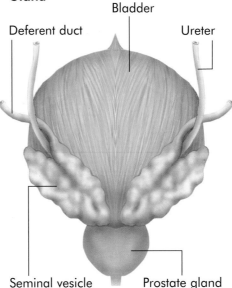

Deferent duct — Bladder — Ureter

Seminal vesicle — Prostate gland

blood from the arteries. The veins (*venae*) that would allow the blood to drain away are closed off, and a congestion of blood is achieved. The penis swells up and becomes erect.

The skin covering the penis contains many muscle cells but no fat cells. It forms a fold at the tip of the penis, the foreskin (prepuce of penis), surrounding the glans. The foreskin is drawn back during an erection, exposing the glans and allowing more effective stimulation.

Structure of the Testicles

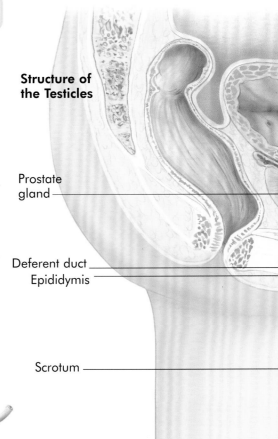

Prostate gland

Deferent duct
Epididymis

Scrotum

Scrotum/Testicles

The scrotum is a bag of skin accommodating the two testicles (*testes*), each of which hangs from a cord. It is situated below the penis and is therefore one of the male external sexual organs.

The egg-shaped, plum-sized testicles, each about 4.0–5.5 cm in size, are the male genital glands (gonads). Their normal position, hanging in the scrotum by the spermatic cords (*funiculus spermaticus*), is assumed just before birth, when they pass through the abdominal wall and inguinal canal.

The fact that the scrotum is situated outside the body results in an internal temperature about

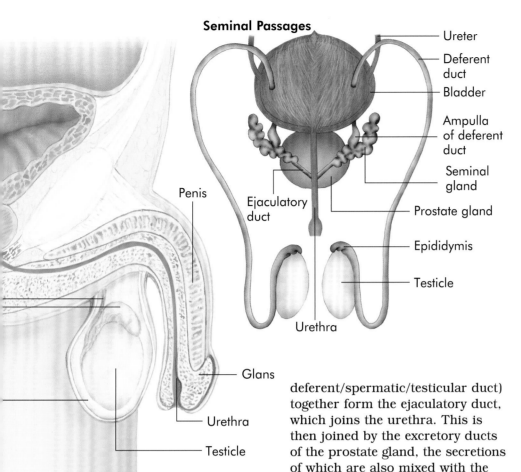

Seminal Passages

- Penis
- Ejaculatory duct
- Urethra
- Glans
- Urethra
- Testicle

- Ureter
- Deferent duct
- Bladder
- Ampulla of deferent duct
- Seminal gland
- Prostate gland
- Epididymis
- Testicle

The penile and urethral cavernous and spongy bodies are filled with blood from the arteries during the first phase. This cannot drain away again because of closure of the appropriate veins. This results in the penis swelling up, becoming hard and erect. The testicles are pulled closer to the body by increased scrotal tension towards the end of the **excitation phase**.

Sexual tension is very high during the **plateau phase**. The penis continues to swell up. The **orgasmic phase** follows. Contraction of the pelvic muscles transports the sperm into the urethra where they are mixed with the seminal fluid from the prostate gland and the seminal vesicle. The spermatic fluid is formed, which is ejaculated into the vagina spasmodically.

The veins are reopened after the orgasm. The congested blood is able to drain away during the **resolution phase**, and the penis relaxes again.

deferent/spermatic/testicular duct) together form the ejaculatory duct, which joins the urethra. This is then joined by the excretory ducts of the prostate gland, the secretions of which are also mixed with the sperm.

3 degrees below normal body temperature. This is advantageous for the production of mature germ cells by the testicles. The second function of the testicles is the formation of testosterone, the male sexual hormone.

The sperm cells produced in each testicle *(didymus)* are stored in the epididymis until full maturity. The epididymis is connected to the deferent duct via the epididymal duct, which is one of two long ducts lined with a muscular layer. The muscular layer of the epididymis contracts during sexual arousal. The suction thereby created allows the sperm to flow out of the epididymis and into the deferent duct via the epididymal duct. The ducts from the seminal gland and the vas deferens (alt.

Sexual Response Cycle

An erection of the male penis is required to allow penetration of the female vagina. Erection may be elicited by physical, psychological or sensory arousal, leading to excitation of the vegetative nervous system.

The cycle of sexual response may be divided in 4 phases:

- **Excitation phase**
- **Plateau phase**
- **Orgasme phase**
- **Resolution phase**

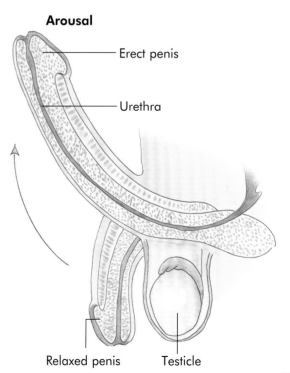

Arousal

- Erect penis
- Urethra
- Relaxed penis
- Testicle

Female Genital Organs

Similar to the male sexual organs, the female genitalia may also be divided into internal and external sexual organs.

The external organs include:
• the large pudendal lips (*labia majora*)
• the small pudendal lips (*labia minora*)
• the clitoris
• the vestibule of the vagina (*vestibulum vaginae*)
• the vestibular gland (Bartholin's gland).

The internal sexual organs are subdivided into:

• the ovaries
• the oviduct (uterine or fallopian tube)
• the uterus (womb)
• the vagina

These allow the fusion of sperm and egg cell, as well as implantation (nidation) after impregnation (fecundation) in the hormonally prepared uterine mucous membrane.

This mucous membrane (endometrium) is maintained in the ensuing months of pregnancy by means of hormone production, in order to allow the development of a new organism capable of life.

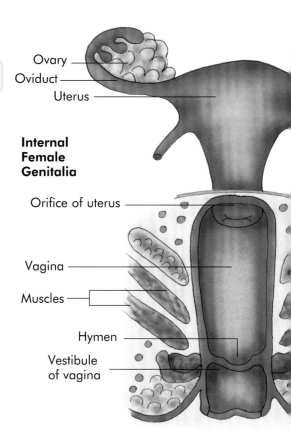

Internal Female Genitalia

Ovary
Oviduct
Uterus
Orifice of uterus
Vagina
Muscles
Hymen
Vestibule of vagina

External Female Genitalia (vulva)

Two large flaps of skin covered with hair, the labia majora, enclose the vaginal vestibule (*vestibulum vaginae*). The two smaller hairless pudendal lips, the labia minora, are located between the larger lips and form a hood towards the front. This almost completely covers the clitoris, with only the tip of the clitoris (glans) exposed. The clitoris is comparable to the penis, since it swells up on being touched.

The vagina, the female urethra (*urethra femina*) and vestibular glands open into the vestibule of the vagina. The vaginal opening (*ostium vaginaie*) is generally almost completely covered by a thin virginal membrane (hymen) before the first sexual intercourse.

The large vestibular glands (*Bartholin's glands*) and various smaller glands (*glandulae vestibulares minores*) of the vaginal vestibule, moisten the entrance of the vagina with their alkaline secretions, thereby facilitating the penetration of the penis.

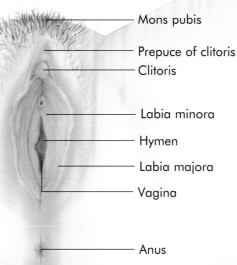

Mons pubis
Prepuce of clitoris
Clitoris
Labia minora
Hymen
Labia majora
Vagina
Anus

Ovaries

In the course of every menstrual cycle (*cyclus menstrualis*), one primary follicle matures to an egg cell (alt. ovum/oocyte/ovocyte) in each ovary and is passed on to the oviduct.

The hormones produced in the process, oestrogen and progesterone (corpus luteum hormone), prepare the uterus for implantation and nourishment of the fertilised egg cell (*zygote*).

The ovaries are connected to the uterus by means of funnel-like structures, the fimbriae of the uterine tubes.

Oviducts
(uterine/fallopian tubes)

The ovum passes into a uterine tube via the fimbriae of the tube (*fimbriae tubae*). The upper section (*ampulla tubae*) of this approximately 10–20 cm-long duct is generally the site of fusion of sperm and ovum.

Glandular secretions accompany the egg cell on its journey. Transport is supported by the fine hairs of the ciliated epithelium as well as by the contraction of the uterine tube muscles towards the uterus.

Uterus

Inside the uterus, there is a thick muscular layer *(myometrium)* and a mucous membrane *(endometrium)*, the thickness of which varies between 2 and 8 mm in the course of every menstrual cycle. If a fertilised egg reaches the uterus, it is taken up by the endometrium and nourished. The muscular layer comes to fulfil its function during the birth process, by contracting, producing labour pains and expelling the baby out of the uterus.

The uterus is divided into body *(corpus uteri)* and neck *(cervix uteri)*. The two oviducts lead into the body of the uterus.

Inside the 2.5 cm-long neck of the womb (or uterus) is a canal linking the uterus with the vagina. The vagina is an approximately 7–10 cm-long tube composed of connective and muscular tissue. It leads from the outer female genital organs to the uterus. Part of the cervix juts into the vagina and is referred to as the vaginal part of the cervix. This has an opening, the external orifice of the uterus *(ostium uteri)*.

Egg Cell *(ovum)*

The egg cell, a spherical cell with a diameter of 0.15 mm, is one of the largest cells of the human body. Similar to the sperm cell, the egg cell has a haploid nucleus with a chromosome set of only 22 chromosomes and 1 sex chromosome.

Insemination of an egg cell by a sperm cell results in a fusion of the nuclei, resulting in the formation of a cell with a diploid, i.e. a complete set of (46) chromosomes.

The nucleus of the ovum lies in the vitellus (yolk) together with the germinal vesicle and the

cortical granules. This is composed of nutrient (deutoplasm) and constructive (protoplasm) material, and forms the cytoplasm. Several protective layers (oolemma) surround the egg.

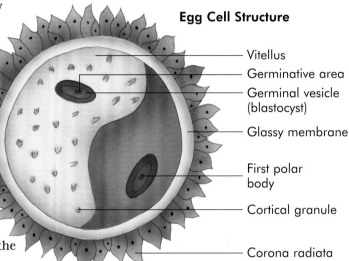

Egg Cell Structure

- Vitellus
- Germinative area
- Germinal vesicle (blastocyst)
- Glassy membrane
- First polar body
- Cortical granule
- Corona radiata

Female Cycle

The hormones oestrogen and progestogen, which are produced in the female ovaries, cause periodic changes to take place in the female body. This repetitive cycle is called the menstrual cycle.

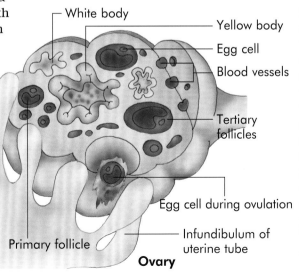

- White body
- Yellow body
- Egg cell
- Blood vessels
- Tertiary follicles
- Egg cell during ovulation
- Primary follicle
- Infundibulum of uterine tube

Ovary

The first menstruation, which generally occurs between the ages of 10 and 16, is known as menarche, while the final menstrual bleeding between the ages of 47 and 52, is called menses.

An average menstrual cycle takes 28 days. During this period, the egg cell is able to pass from the ovary to the oviduct during the process of ovulation. At the same time, the endometrium becomes thicker due to an increased secretion of progesterone (a progestogen or gestagen) and is thereby prepared for the event of possible fertilisation. If this does not take place, then the endometrium is detached and flushed out of the vagina together with the egg cell, in the form of the regular process of menstrual bleeding or 'the period'. A follicle develops in the ovary again once the bleeding stops.

Sexual Response Cycle

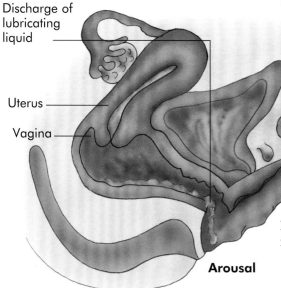

Discharge of lubricating liquid

Uterus

Vagina

Arousal

The female cycle of sexual response may also be divided into 4 phases, just like the male cycle.

The **excitation phase** is initiated by stimulation of the clitoris. The outer genital organs *(organa genitalia feminina)* are perfused with more blood than normally, the nipples *(mamilae)* become erect and the breasts *(mammae)* swell. Inside the vagina, the glands of the vaginal mucous membrane discharge a secretion that facilitates penetration of the penis.

The **plateau phase** involves the lower part of the vagina becoming narrower due to the vaginal wall swelling, while the upper part becomes wider. The narrower vagina, having more intimate contact with the penis, allows better stimulation.

As far as the outer genital organs are concerned, the labia majora become more swollen, the labia minora become red in colour and the clitoris retracts. The uterus assumes a vertical position. The vaginal muscles contract during the **orgasmic phase**. The **resolution phase** follows the orgasm.

Reproduction

Human reproduction takes place by means of the genital organs. This involves the fusion of two germ cells (gametes), one male and one female.

The male germ cell is the sperm and the female germ cell is the ovum. The nucleus of each contains half a chromosome complement (haploid set) bearing the hereditary information (genes) for the new individual. If the sperm and egg cells are united, i.e. conception (insemination/fecundation) takes place, then the nuclei fuse, the maternal and paternal chromosomes are mixed and a new cell is produced with a complete number of chromosomes (diploid set), which represents the foundation of new life.

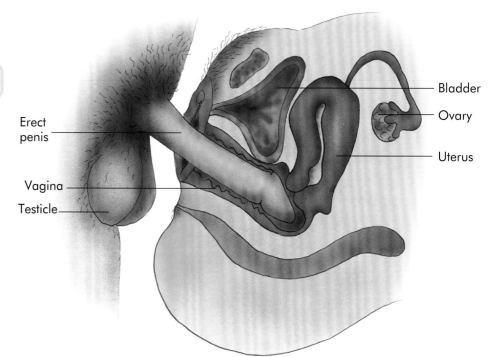

Erect penis

Vagina

Testicle

Bladder

Ovary

Uterus

Sexual Intercourse

In order to make the unification of sperm and egg cell, and thus ultimately reproduction, possible, it is necessary to introduce the man's erect penis into the vagina of the woman.

An ejaculation will result in the sperm reaching the uterus after passing through the vagina, into the opening of the uterus *(ostium uteri)* and the neck of the uterus *(cervix uteri)*. The sperm are transported to the oviducts from there.

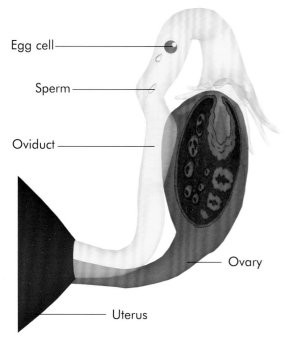

Egg cell

Sperm

Oviduct

Ovary

Uterus

Insemination
(fecundatio)

Insemination is only possible at the time of ovulation, which is roughly between the 14th and 15th day of the menstrual cycle.

The egg cell can be fertilised for about 6–12 hours after leaving the ovary; it is destroyed after that time. Fertilisation takes place in the upper part of the oviduct, the ampulla of the uterine tube.

The spermatozoon penetrates the ovum up to its midpiece, while the flagellum (tail) is discarded.

The head of the sperm cell swells and forms the male pronucleus. The egg cell is still engaged in the second phase of division during the process of sperm penetration. The ovarian nucleus also swells up and forms the female pronucleus.

The fusion of the two nuclei results in a cell with 46 chromosomes (diploid nucleus), the fertilised egg cell. This is the basis for the development of a new human being.

Fertilisation of Ovum, Development of Morula and Blastocyst

Released ovum

Fertilised ovum

Zygote formed by the fusion of egg and sperm cells

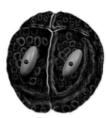

Zygote, divided into 4 blastomeres

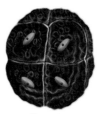

Zygote, divided into 8 blastomeres

Morula on about the 4th day after fertilisation

Chromosome Division and Implantation

The fertilised egg cell (zygote) travels from the oviduct toward the uterus. En route, it divides into about 16 smaller cells, the blastomeres, by rapid mitotic division. These get smaller with each division, since their growth is temporarily halted. The blastomeres finally form a morula, a cell structure whose name refers to its similarity to a mulberry. It is also known as berry cell.

The morula enters the uterus about one week after insemination. Its interior slowly fills with liquid,

in a manner allowing another hollow cavity to be formed after four days.

The morula is now referred to as a blastocyst. At the beginning of the second week of pregnancy, the outer cells of the blastocyst form a layer called the trophoblast, while the inner cells form a mass of cells called the embryoblast. The embryo will develop from this structure in the course of pregnancy.

The trophoblast sinks into the uterine mucous membrane *(tunica mucosa)* and forms outpockets known as cotyledons. These cotyledons represent the connection between the foetal blood vessels and the uterine blood vessels.

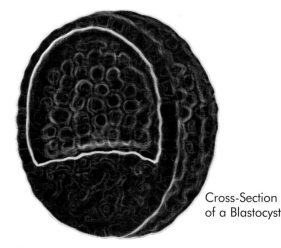

Cross-Section of a Blastocyst

If a released egg cell is inseminated by a sperm, a zygoteforms. Cell division already commences while the zygote is on its way to the uterus. After various stages, in the process of which the zygote is divided into 4, 8 and 16 blastomeres, a segmentation sphere is obtained, the morula, hardly larger than the fertilised egg cell. The egg reaches the uterus at this stage, on about the 4th day.

Pregnancy

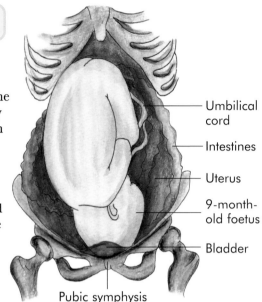

Pregnancy (gravidity) commences with the impregnation of the egg cell by a sperm. In the course of a pregnancy, this fertilised egg cell develops into a foetus within the uterus, which inevitably leads to changes in the female body.

The other internal organs are displaced due to the pressure of a growing uterus. Breathing becomes more difficult for the pregnant woman, and vascular circulation may also be affected.

The pregnancy culminates with the birth of a baby. A normal pregnancy takes an average of 9 months, which is approximately 38–40 weeks.

If the time of the last menstruation and therefore also the time of ovulation is unknown, then it is also possible to calculate the period of duration of the pregnancy on the basis of the size of the uterus.

Umbilical cord

Intestines

Uterus

9-month-old foetus

Bladder

Pubic symphysis

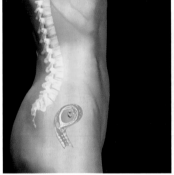

1ˢᵗ month
1–2 g
0,75 cm

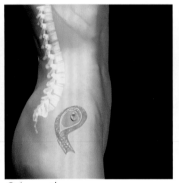

2ⁿᵈ month
5–8 g
3 cm

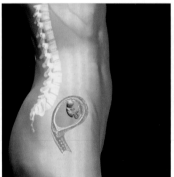

3ʳᵈ month
18–20 g
15 cm

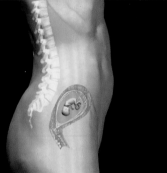

4ᵗʰ month
120 g
21 cm

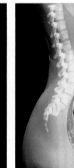

5ᵗʰ month
300 g
27 cm

Embryonic Development

From the inner cells of the blastocyst, the inner germ layer develops into the entoderm, while the outer germ layer forms the ectoderm. During the third week of pregnancy, a germ layer between these two develops, the mesoderm. The foetal organs are formed from these three germ layers. Two small cavities are also formed, one near the ectoderm and one near the endoderm.

The ectodermal cavity is called the amniotic cavity, into which the embryo will grow during the further course of pregnancy. It is filled with amniotic fluid, protecting the embryo from blows. The entodermal cavity, the umbilical vesicle (or yolk sac), slowly deteriorates.

The embryo is already 7 mm long and weighs 1 g by the end of the fourth week of pregnancy. The development of the heart, the spinal column, the central nervous system, the head and the brain begins.

The foundations of all the important organs, such as the digestive tract and the respiratory centre, are established during the second month of pregnancy. The heart of the embryo begins to beat as early as the fifth week of pregnancy.

The embryo has assumed a human appearance by the end of the second month of pregnancy. Rudimentary sensory organs have developed from small depressions and vaults, with the eyes being almost completely formed. The head and brain grow faster in comparison with the rest of the body. The extremities with the associated fingers and toes are recognisable and are already capable of movement, which is however not perceived by the mother.

Foetal Development

The foetal phase begins on the 85th day of pregnancy. The embryo is now referred to as foetus (Latin for 'young one'). The progress of development of the brain, face, cardiovascular system and limbs is slower at this stage, in contrast to the following months.

By the end of the twelfth week, the foetus weighs about 20 g and is approximately 15 cm long. The cardiovascular system is fully functional and the brain is almost completely developed. The increased movement of arms and legs still cannot be detected by the mother.

An accelerated growth period begins during the fourth month of pregnancy and continues until the end of the seventh month. The foetus is covered with very fine down-like hair *(lanugo)*. The finger and toe nails are formed.

The kidneys commence their production of urine at the beginning of the fifth month of pregnancy. The limbs are now capable of significant movement. The foetus weighs about 300 g and is approximately 25 cm long. The muscular system is almost completely developed by the end of the 6th month. Although organ development progresses rapidly, the chance of survival of a foetus at the end of the seventh month of pregnancy is as little as 5%. A maximal growth period starts with the 27th week of pregnancy, continuing until the 37th week.

The organs then complete their development. The foetus gets ready for birth and turns upside down (cephalic presentation). By the end of the ninth month, the foetus weighs approximately 3,500 g and is about 50 cm long.

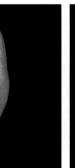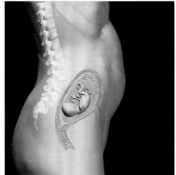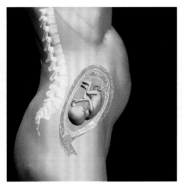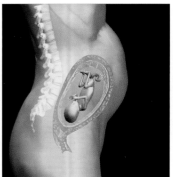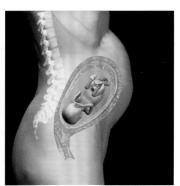

6th month
800–900 g
33 cm

7th month
1300–1400 g
39 cm

8th month
2200–2300 g
45 cm

9th month
3200–3500 g
48–51 cm

Placenta *(placenta)*

The function of the placenta is to allow an exchange of substances between mother and offspring throughout pregnancy, thereby enabling its nourishment. It represents the liver, intestines and kidneys of the embryo/foetus until birth. The placenta is in a position to carry out all of its functions without any restrictions from about the twelfth month of pregnancy.

The maternal and foetal blood vessels remain separate from each other, in order to prevent the entry of any harmful substances. This however excludes the viruses causing rubella and toxoplasmosis, as well as drugs such as alcohol or nicotine that may be contained in the mother's blood.

The placenta is connected to the embryo/foetus by means of an umbilical cord *(funiculus umbilicalis)* approximately 1 metre in length, composed of connective tissue. Located in the cord are the umbilical vein *(vena umbilicalis)* and the umbilical artery *(arteria umbilicales)*.

The placenta moreover produces a number of hormones, which for instance prevent the formation of new egg cells in the ovaries and stimulate uterine growth and the production of milk by the mammary glands in the female breast *(mamma)* in the further course of pregnancy.

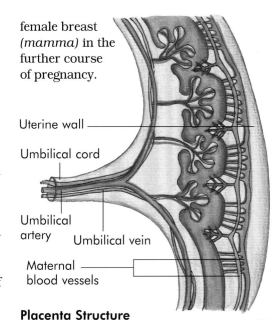

Uterine wall

Umbilical cord

Umbilical artery   Umbilical vein

Maternal blood vessels

Placenta Structure

Birth

Birth begins with the labour pains, the contractions of the muscles of the uterine mucous membrane *(tunica mucosa)*.

Contractions are felt at intervals of about thirty minutes at the start of the birth process. The intervals become increasingly smaller (about 2–3 minutes) while the duration of each contraction becomes longer.

False labour pains are common before the actual birth process, but these occur at non-periodic intervals and only last a few seconds.

Childbirth (parturition) is divided into three phases:
• **dilation stage** (1st stage of labour)
• **expulsion stage** (2nd stage of labour)
• **placental stage** (3rd stage of labour)

The duration of each of these stages depends on various factors. This includes the duration of the individual contractions, the ability of the mouth of the uterus *(ostium uteri)* to dilate and the number of preceding deliveries (first or successive birth).

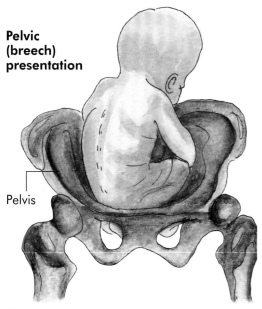

Pelvic (breech) presentation

Pelvis

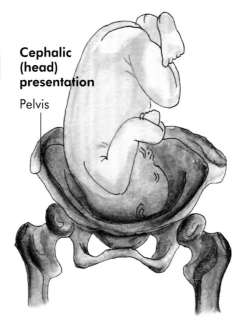

Cephalic (head) presentation

Pelvis

Foetal Presentation

The foetus is about 50 cm long towards the end of the term of pregnancy, almost completely filling the uterus, which extends from the pelvis to the breastbone (sternum) of the mother at this stage.

The space available for the foetus becomes increasingly tight and it is hardly able to move its limbs. This results in the adoption of the position that will also facilitate its departure from the maternal body through the narrow birth canal in the course of the birth process. Its arms and legs are hugged closely to the bent body, in a position generally known as the foetal position.

The foetus begins to turn during the 36th week of pregnancy, so that, ideally, by the end of the pregnancy term, its head is facing downwards and its bottom is facing upwards – 'ready to go' in a head presentation. This cephalic presentation, also referred to as vertex presentation, with the crown (vertex) of the foetal head facing in direction cervix, is the normal foetal presentation.

The pelvic or breech presentation, i.e. with the foetus' bottom located in the pelvis, can make the birth process more difficult, since, instead of the head, the feet or bottom will have to pass through the birth canal first.

Dilation Stage

The commencement of labour pains initiates the first stage of labour, the stage of dilation. The amniotic sac, filled with amniotic fluid, bulges in front of the foetal head situated in the pelvis. The contractions repeatedly push the foetal head against the neck of the womb, resulting in the gradual dilation of the uterine neck. The amniotic sac can be compared to a shock absorber during this process.

The stage of dilation is completed once a dilation from 3 cm to 10 cm of the cervix (or neck of the uterus) and the adjoining uterine orifice has been achieved. The pressure of the foetal head on the amniotic sac leads to amniorrhexis, the rupture of the amniotic sac. The amniotic fluid (or 'the waters') drain out and the stage of expulsion begins.

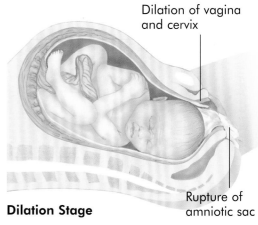

Dilation of vagina and cervix

Dilation Stage

Rupture of amniotic sac

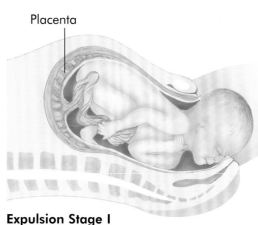

Placenta

Expulsion Stage I

Explusion Stage

At the beginning of this second stage of labour, the stage of expulsion, the mother feels the urge to push the baby out of her body by pressing. Further and increasingly severe contractions of the uterine musculature, the second-stage contractions also called bearing down pains or pushing contractions, ensure that a shortening of the musculature occurs. The uterus consequently contracts and the foetus is pushed forwards, towards the pelvic inlet. The head of the child now turns from the longitudinal position adopted so far to a transverse position, i.e. the face is turned to the side in order to pass through the transverse oval aperture of the pelvic inlet and enter the pelvic canal. The pelvic outlet on the other hand has a longitudinal oval opening, and this is why the foetal head turns 90 degrees back to the longitudinal position on its way through the pelvic canal, emerging from the vaginal opening with the back of the head first. The now-delivered head needs to make another 90 degree turn, assisted by an obstetrician or a midwife, since the shoulders of the baby now follow, also passing the pelvic outlet in a longitudinal position. The shoulders are born one after the other. The rest of the body is smaller in comparison to the head. This allows the rib cage, pelvis and legs to slide through the pre-stretched birth canal very quickly. The umbilical cord still connecting the newborn to the placenta at this stage is severed.

Pushing contractions

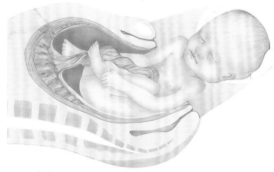

Expulsion Stage II

Placenta

Umbilical cord

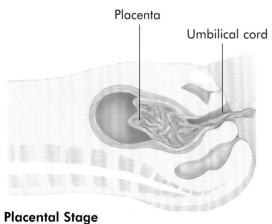

Placental Stage

Placental Stage

The third stage of labour, the placental stage, begins immediately after the emergence of the baby from the mother's body. The uterus contracts further, resulting in the placenta becoming detached from the endometrium. This process may take up to half an hour. Slight afterpains commence and the afterbirth, composed of placenta, the amniotic sac membrane and the umbilical cord, is finally expelled with a single pushing contraction. The birth process is now complete and the mother is now referred to as a woman in childbed (puerpera).

Childbed

The postnatal period of time required to allow the organs to return to normality is called lying-in or the childbed period *(puerperium)*.

The uterus, which weighs about 1 kg at the end of pregnancy, has regained its normal weight of 60 g after about 4–6 weeks.

The damage incurred by the blood vessels inside the uterus due to the detachment of the placenta from the endometrium during the placental stage heals. The discharge that arises in the course of this process is referred to as lochia. This is relatively profuse during the first days after birth. It is chiefly composed of red blood cells *(erythrocytes)* and is therefore also called lochia rubra. After about three days, this becomes lighter in colour (lochia serosa) due to the high proportion of white blood cells (leukocytes). When the blood vessels have finally healed after about one week, the discharge becomes thin and watery (lochia alba). It takes about 30 days for the lochia to stop.

The maternal hormone balance changes significantly after delivery. A greater amount of the hormone prolactin, which stimulates milk production (lactation) in the mammary glands, is produced. The mammary glands produce so-called foremilk (colostrum), which was formed during the final months of pregnancy. This contains less fat than the milk produced subsequently. Milk is produced as long as breastfeeding is continued regularly.

INDEX

A

Abdominal Muscles 12
Accommodation 66, 67
Achilles Tendon 13
Adrenal Cortex 50
Adrenal Glands 50, 51
Adrenal Medulla 50
Adrenaline 50
Afterbirth 93
Aldosterone 50, 53
Alimentary Tract, lower 38
Alimentary Tract, upper 34
Alveoli 19
Amniotic Sac 92
Amylase 36
Anaphase 80, 81
Androgens 51
Ankle Joint 9
Anvil 65
Aorta 23, 45
Appendix 38, 41
Aqueous Humour 66
Arachnoid Membrane 57
Arm Muscle 12
Arteries 26, 29, 30
Assimilatory Metabolism 81
Astigmatism 67
Atria 22, 23, 24
Atrioventricular Valves 24, 25
Auditory Canal, external 65
Auditory Nerve 65
Auditory Tube 65
Auricle 65
Axon 59

B

Back Muscles 13
Bile Formation 43
Birth 92, 93
Bladder 44, 74, 75, 84, 88
Blind Spot 66
Blood 81
Blood Circulation 22, 26
Blood Vessels 29
Body of Uterus 87
Bone Formation 9
Bone Marrow 8
Bone Structure 8
Bone/Cartilage 8, 9
Bowman's Capsule 73
Brachial Muscle 13
Brain 56, 57, 60
Brainstem 56, 57
Breastbone 11
Bronchi 19
Bronchioles 19

C

Caecum 38, 41
Calcium 49
Canine Teeth 34
Capillaries 26, 29, 31
Capillary System, double 27
Carbohydrate Metabolism 43
Carbohydrates 42
Cardiac Circulation 28
Cardiac Muscle System 12
Cardiovalvular System 24, 25
Carotid Artery 22, 48
Carpal Bones of the Wrist 11
Cartilage of Nasal Septum 16
Cartilage Ring, C-shaped 18
Cartilage, elastic 8
Cartilage, hyaline 8
Cartilaginous Tissue 8
Cavernous Body of Penis 75, 84
Cell Body 59
Cell Nucleus 59, 77, 79
Central Nervous System 56
Centrioles 78
Cerebellum 53, 56, 57
Cerebrospinal Fluid 56, 57
Cerebrum 53, 56
Cervical Vertebra 10
Cheek Bone 10
Childbed 93
Chromatin 79, 80
Chromosome Complement 79, 80
Chromosome Division 89
Chromosomes 79, 80
Clavicle 11
Clitoris 86
Coccyx 10, 11
Cochlea 65
Colon 41
Compact Bone 8
Cornea 66
Corona Radiata 87
Coronary Vessels 23, 25
Cortical Granule 87
Cortisol 50
Costal Cartilage 11
Cowper's Gland 75
Cranium 10
Cricoid Cartilage 16, 18
Cytoplasm 77, 78

D

Deferent Duct 52, 84
Deltoid Muscle 12, 13
Dendrites 59
Dental Crown 35
Dental Root 35

Dentine 35
Dermis 64
Detoxification 43
Diabetes 51
Diaphragm 17, 19, 44
Diencephalon (Interbrain) 56
Dietary Fibre 40
Dissimilatory Metabolism 81
DNA Chain 81
DNA Replication 80
DNA Structure 80, 81
Duodenal Papilla 44
Duodenum 38, 40, 41, 44, 45

E

Ear 63, 65
Egg Cell 87, 89
Elbow Joint 9
Embryonic Development 90
Endocrine Tissue 53
Endolymph 65
Endoplasmic Reticulum 78
Epidermis 64
Epididymis 52, 84, 85
Epiglottis 16, 17, 18, 37
Erection 84
Ethmoid Bone 10
Extensor Muscle of Finger 13
Extensor Retinaculum 20
Extremities, lower 11
Extremities, upper 11
Eye Muscles 67
Eyeball 66
Eyes 63, 66

F

Fallopian Tube 52, 86, 87, 89
Farsightedness 67
Femoral Muscle 12
Femur 11
Fertilisation 89
Fibrous Cartilage 8
Fibula 11
Finger Bone 11
Flexor Muscle of Finger 12
Flexor Muscle of Foot 12
Flexor Muscles of Toes 12
Foetal Development 91
Foetal Presentation 92
Follicular Cells 52
Forehead Muscle 12
Foreskin 84
Frontal Bone 10, 66
Frontal Sinus 60

G

Gall Bladder 38, 42, 44, 45
Gastric Mucous Membrane 39
Gastrin 39, 53
Gastrocnemius (Calf) Muscle 13
Genes 80, 88
Genital Glands 52
Genital Organs, female 85–86
Genital Organs, male 84–85
Germinal Vesicle 87
Germinative Area 87
Glands, digestive system 42
Glands, endocrine 42, 49
Glands, exocrine 42
Glans 75, 84
Glassy Membrane 87
Glottal Aperture 16, 18
Glucose 42, 51
Gluteal Muscle 13
Golgi Body 78
Grey Matter 57
Gums 35
Gustatory System 68

H

Hair Sheath 64
Hammer 65
Haversian Canals 8
Haversian System 8
Hearing and Balance 65
Heart 22, 23, 26
Hemispheres 56
Hepatic Lobules 43
Hip Bone 11
Humerus 11
Hymen 86
Hyoid Bone 16, 34
Hyperthyroidism 48
Hypodermis 64
Hypothyroidism 48

I

Ileum 38, 41
Iliac Bone 11
Implantation 89
Incisors 34
Infraspinatus Muscle 13
Insemination 89
Insulin 51
Interventricular Septum 22
Intervertebral Disks 10
Intestinal Mucosa 40
Intestinal Villi 40
Intestines 39, 40, 41
Iris 66
Ischial Bone 11
Islets of Langerhans 51

J

Jejenum 38, 39, 41

K

Kidneys 72, 73
Knee Joint 9
Krause's Corpuscles 64

L

Labia 86
Labour Pains 87, 92
Lacrimal Bone 10
Large Intestine 38, 40, 41, 44
Laryngeal Pharynx 17
Larynx 17, 18, 19, 37
Lens 66
Leydig's Cells 52
Lingual Frenulum 34
Lipid Metabolism 43
Lipids 39, 42, 43
Lips 34
Liver 38, 42, 43, 44
Lower Jaw 10, 16, 34
Lumbar Vertebra 10
Lumbosacral Joint 10
Lung, left, right 19
Lungs 17, 18, 19
Lysosomes 78
Lysozyme 36

Joints 9
Jugular Vein 48

M

Malleus 65
Medulla Oblongata 56
Meiosis 77, 79
Meissner's Corpuscles 64
Melatonin 53
Meninges 57
Menstrual Cycle 87, 89
Mesencephalon 56
Mesentery 44
Metabolism 81
Metacarpal Bones 11
Metaphase 80, 81
Metaplasm 78
Mitochondria 78
Mitosis 77, 80
Molars 35
Mouth 34
Muscle Function 13
Muscle Slings 7
Muscles, smooth 12
Muscles, striated 12
Musculature 12, 13
Myelin Sheath 59

N

Nasal Bone 10, 16
Nasal Cavity 16
Nasal Concha 10, 16

Nasal Septum 10, 17
Nasopharynx 16, 17
Neck of Uterus 87
Nephron 73, 74
Nerve Cell 59
Nerve Control 60
Nerve Fibres 59
Nerves 58
Noradrenaline 50
Nose 63
Nucleolus 79
Nuclear Membrane 79
Nucleoplasm 79
Nucleotides 80

O

Occipital Muscle 13
Oesophagus 16, 17, 37
Oestrogen 51, 52, 86
Olfactory Cells 69
Olfactory Knob 16, 69
Olfactory Mucosa 16, 69
Olfactory Nerve 69
Olfactory System 69
Omentum, greater 44
Optic Chiasm 53
Orbicular Muscle of Eye 12
Orbicular Muscle of Mouth 12
Orgasm 85, 88
Oropharynx 17
Oval Fossa 22
Ovaries 52, 86
Oviduct 52, 86, 87, 89

P

Pain Receptor 64
Palate 34
Palate Bone 16
Palatine Tonsil 17, 34
Palatine Velum 34
Pancreas 38, 42, 44, 45, 51
Pancreozymin 53
Papillary Muscles 22
Paraplasm 78
Parasympathetic Nervous System 58
Parathyroid Glands 49
Parathyroid Hormone 49
Parietal Bone 10
Parotid Gland 36
Patella 11
Pelvic Girdle 11
Pelvis 11
Penis 75, 84, 88
Pepsin 39
Periosteum 8
Peripheral Nervous System 58, 59
Peristalsis 37
Phagocytosis 81
Pharyngeal Tonsil 17
Pharynx 16, 17, 34, 37
Pineal Gland 53
Pituitary Gland 53, 56

Placenta 91
Placental Structure 91
Polar Body 87
Pons 53, 56
Portal Vein 27, 28
Primary Urine 73
Pregnancy 90
Presbyopia 67
Primary Bronchus 19
Primary Follicle 87
Progesterone 86
Progestogen/Gestagen 51
Prophase 80
Prostate Gland 75, 84
Protein Metabolism 43
Proteins 39, 42, 43
Pubic Bone 11
Pubic Symphysis 11
Pulmonary Artery 23
Pulmonary Capillary Network 19
Pulmonary Circulation 26, 28
Pulmonary Valve 22, 28
Pulmonary Veins 22
Pupil 66
Pyramidal Lobes 48

R

Radius 11
Receptors 64
Rectum 38, 41, 45
Reflex Arc 61
Reflexes 61
Renal Calice 72
Renal Capsule 72
Renal Corpuscles 72, 73
Renal Cortex 72
Renal Medulla 72
Renal Pelvis 72
Renal Tubules 73
Renin 53
Reproduction 88
Respiratory Passages 16
Respiratory Passages, lower 17
Retina 66, 67
Ribosomes 78
Ribs 17
Ribs (1st–12th) 11
Ruffini's Corpuscles 64

S

Sacrum 10, 11
Saliva 36
Salivary Glands 36
Schwann Cell 59
Scrotum 84, 85
Semicircular Canals 65
Semilunar Cusps 24, 25
Seminal Passages 85
Seminal Vesicles 75, 84
Semitendinous Muscle 13
Sexual Intercourse 88
Sexual Response Cycle, female 88
Sexual Response Cycle, male 85

Shortsightedness 67
Shoulder Blade 11
Shoulder Joint 9
Sinoatrial Node 23
Skeleton 10, 11
Skin 63, 64
Small Intestine 38, 39, 41, 44
Smell 69
Sodium Ions 50
Soft Palate 17
Sound Waves 65
Sperm 85, 88, 89
Spermatocytes 85
Sphenoid Bone 10
Spinal Column 10, 17, 45
Spinal Cord 57
Spinal Meninx 57
Spinal Nerves 57
Spongy Body of Male Urethra 75, 84
Spongy Bone 8
Sternal Manubrium 11
Sternocleidomastoideus Muscle 12
Stimulus and Pain 60, 61
Stirrup Bone 67
Stomach 38, 39, 44
Stool 41
Sublingual Gland 36
Submandibular Gland 36
Swallowing Act 34
Swallowing Process 36, 37
Sweat Gland 64
Sympathetic Nervous System 85
Systemic Circulation 26, 27, 28

T

Tailor's Muscle (Sartorius) 12
Taste Buds 35, 68
Taste Cells 68
Taste Perception 68
Teeth 10, 34, 35
Telophase 80, 81
Temporal Bone 10
Tendinous Cords 22
Teres Muscle 13
Tertiary Follicle 87
Testicles 52, 84, 85
Testosterone 52, 85
Thalamus 53
Thoracic Muscle 12
Thoracic Vertebra 10
Thorax 11, 17
Thyroid Cartilage 16, 18, 48
Thyroid Follicle 48, 49
Thyroid Gland 48
Thyroxine 48
Thyroxine-producing Cells 49
Tibia 11
Tongue 16, 34, 35, 63
Tooth Cement 35
Tooth Enamel 35
Tooth Pulp 35
Touch 64
Trachea 16, 17, 18, 19
Trapezoid Muscle 12, 13

Triiodothyronine 48
Tubular Bone 8
Tympanic Cavity 65
Tympanum (Ear Drum) 65

U

Ulna 11
Upper Jaw 10, 16, 34
Ureter 74
Urethra, female 75
Urethra, male 75
Urine 74
Uriniferous Tubules 72, 73
Uterus 52, 75, 87, 88
Uvula 17, 34

V

Vagina 86, 88
Vaginal Vestibule 86
Vater-Pacini Corpuscles 64
Vegetative Nervous System 58
Veins 26, 29, 31
Vena Cava, inferior 22
Vena Cava, superior 22
Venous Valves 30, 31
Ventricles 22, 23, 24
Vermiform Appendage 38
Vestibular Nerve 65
Vestibular Sacs utricule and saccule 65
Vision 66, 67
Visual Defects 67
Visual Pathway 66
Vitellus 87
Vitreous Humour 66
Vocal Cords 18

W

White Body 87
White Matter 57
Window, Oval 65
Window, Round 65
Wrist 9
Wrist Extensor 13
Wrist Flexor 12

X

Xyphoid Process 11

Y

Yellow Body 87
Yellow Spot 66

Picture credits
Fotolia.com: pp. 6 (© PIC4U), 14 (© magicmine), 20 (© yodiyim), 32 (© magicmine), 46 (© nerthuz), 54 (© PIC4U), 62 (© reineg), 70 (© 7activestudio), 76 (© Wire_man), 82 (© newrossosh)
All other images: the contmedia GmbH archive